MANSFIELD PARK

MANSFIELD PARK

❖

PATRICIA ROZEMA

FINAL SHOOTING SCRIPT

**talk
miramax
books**
NEW YORK

Library of Congress Cataloging-in-Publication Data

ISBN: 0-7868-8603-X

FIRST EDITION

10 9 8 7 6 5 4 3 2 1

MANSFIELD PARK

A C K N O W L E D G M E N T S

I would like to thank David Aukin, Alon Reich, Sarah Curtis, Julie Goldstein, Jack Lechner, Harvey Weinstein, Lesley Barber and Jacoba Rozema for their taste and their tolerance.

INTRODUCTION

Jane Austen's popularity at the movies during the past half decade or so has been so stunning and so conspicuous that it is tempting to overlook how often her novels have been adapted for television, for radio, for the stage, and even for the big screen in the past. While we're busy celebrating the "Austen renaissance" of the 1990s, we forget that ever since the 1950s, the BBC has adapted her novels for television virtually every decade. Because Austen is among the English-speaking world's most beloved authors, revered as much by common readers as by scholars, she is never very far from the public's imagination. Accordingly, adaptations of her novels have inevitably—and appropriately—told us as much about what is on our minds at the time as they have about the novels themselves. The first movie of an Austen novel—MGM's classic production of *Pride and Prejudice*—appeared in 1940, when England, standing alone against Germany, was suffering grievously from bombing attacks, and when its very survival looked bleak.

By today's standards of fidelity—whether we call them responsibly scru-pulous or slavishly literal-minded—the MGM *Pride and Prejudice* is absurd. Of course, screen adaptations are always reinventions, and depart radically from their source, if only because novels, unlike movies, can simply tell us charac-ters' unspoken thoughts and feelings that movies must convey visually; and because movies must drastically cut, condense, and consolidate the material more expansively described in novels. This, in order to come in at around one hundred minutes, the typical length of a feature film. But even allowing for inevitable divergences, the MGM *Pride and Prejudice*, starring Laurence Olivier and Greer Garson, seems particularly cavalier about fidelity to the original text. Set merely in "olde England," it features fashions from the Amer-ican antebellum South; because the Hollywood Production Code expressly forbids the ridicule of clergymen, Mr. Collins is cast as a librarian; and Lady Catherine herself turns out to be a swell old gal who only *pretends* to be tyrannical in order to test Darcy's character! Yet despite these departures, this screen version of *Pride and Prejudice* strikes me as not only impressive but moving. For English audiences, hammered by the Blitz, the escape offered by the movie's marriage plot must have seemed consoling and inspiriting in its promise of civility and repose; and for U.S. audiences wary about entering the war at all, *Pride and Prejudice*—like *Mrs. Miniver* (1942) if less dramatically—presented England not as entrenched in effete and moribund class structures, but as domestic and accommodating, as endearing as well as spunky, as a sister nation worthy and needful of our alliance.

Patricia Rozema's production of *Mansfield Park* (1999) is much more care-ful about the demands of historical accuracy than the 1940 *Pride and Prejudice*. But it shares with this first Austen movie an interest not simply in representing an Austen novel, but in engaging creatively with that novel in order to explore how and what Austen teaches us across the span of nearly two centuries. Whereas the first finds brightness in our darkest hour, Rozema's movie ad-dresses the dark side of our prosperity. Who, it asks, is paying for our party?

By foregrounding the troubling elements of Austen's world instead of its charms, Rozema's *Mansfield Park* is true to the novel. Following upon the success of *Pride and Prejudice*, which Austen herself described as "too light and bright and sparkling," *Mansfield Park* turns ambitiously to weightier and serious matters. In honoring the marked seriousness of Austen's novel, however, Ro-zema's movie runs counter to a nostalgic and idealizing pattern established in recent adaptations. Many recent Austen movies have been in their own ways formidable achievements: the Ang Lee/Emma Thompson *Sense and Sensibility* (1995), for example, splendidly conjures the sufferings of love; and Roger Mitchell's *Persuasion* (1995) foreswears glamor for the understated, deep, and at times despairing yearning so remarkable in that novel. But even while these movies convey the trenchancy of Austen's criticism about the manners of her age and its pursuit of wealth and status at the expense of intelligence and sincerity, their loving attention to decor and costume carries us in a different direction, supporting an elegiac tendency to celebrate the manners and the material splendor of Austen's world, a tendency that reigns supreme in the 1995 A&E/BBC version of *Pride and Prejudice*. As our own prosperity has increased, and as Austen movies themselves have become a real phenomenon, they have inflated coziness into opulence: costumes have become more lavish, and country houses grandiose. Austen's novels themselves are typically indifferent to such matters. Far from lingering over the tea sets and the furnishings of manor houses and the fashions favored by the men and women living in them, Austen almost never mentions them at all. Her women and men are incomparably vivid to us, but we are very rarely told what they look like, much less about the clothing they wear or the rooms they occupy.

By their very nature as a visual medium, movies give a prominence to physical detail not present in the novels themselves. And Rozema's *Mansfield Park* is quite remarkable for its effort to cut back on the lavishness of the setting, preferring a sparer and less distracting look. In part this is a gesture of faithfulness to Austen's novel, as we have seen, and also to her historical period, for the interiors of Regency manor houses were in fact far less crowded and plush than their Victorian counterparts. But the spareness of Rozema's film is also an interpretative move. Her cinematographer is Michael Coulter, who also shot the Lee/Thompson *Sense and Sensibility,* with its rich blues and penchant for the spectacular and the sumptuous. Unlike it, *Mansfield Park* is shot mostly in cream and yellow tones, and purposefully avoids being seductive to the eye. In contrast to other directors, Rozema resists the camera's tendency to glamorize the country estate or to celebrate its supposed comforts by picturing them richly. Sensibly, she chose a manor house much less inviting for her setting: Kirby Hall in Northamptonshire, currently maintained by the English Heritage. Having visited scores of stately homes so brimful of furniture that it would have exceeded her budget just to empty them, much less to redecorate them for filming, Rozema found Kirby Hall perfect for her purposes. Built in 1570 and abandoned in 1810 because (it is thought) of massive gambling debts—one thinks of Austen's novel, where Tom's mounting gambling debts alarm Sir Thomas—Kirby Hall is a ruin, inhabited today solely by peacocks. In the movie, it looks cold, drafty, and in manifest disrepair, and these details work, for Mansfield Park is not like that famously venerable and attractive estate, Pemberley, described with rapt and loving attention in *Pride and Prejudice*. Indeed, in several places the novel suggests that Mansfield Park, supported by new money, is on the skids—the care of a little girl like Fanny is an expense Sir Thomas must think twice about—and before long we realize that something is wrong at Mansfield Park.

Why is the country house crumbling? Why are the adults so lacking in moral fiber, and the children so wayward? To answer these questions, we must address a subject that some read Austen precisely to avoid: politics. In a haunting early scene, young Fanny, torn from her family to be treated as a semi-menial among affluent relations, hears a wailing song from a ship off the coast. "Black cargo," the coachman informs her. The comforts of Fanny's new home, we learn, come from slave labor on plantations owned in Antigua by Fanny's uncle Sir Thomas. Foregrounding this element of the novel, Rozema draws on Austen's well-known attachment to fervent and eminent abolitionist writers—such as Samuel Johnson and William Cowper (writers who are Fanny's favorites too, incidentally) and Thomas Clarkson, an abolitionist Austen described herself as in love with.

Because Rozema's attention to the place slavery holds in Austen's novel and during her time in general has struck some as inappropriate or anachronistic, it is important to bear in mind that Austen was more unblinking and engaged than her latter-day, elegiac admirers have often given her credit for. Austen's own father was a trustee of an Antiguan plantation, and such was the dependence of the English economy on the sugar grown in its West Indian plantations; most gentry families during the period had some connection with slavery. Abolishing the slave trade was among the most momentous events of Austen's lifetime, and by the time Parliament voted to do so in 1807—and let's not forget that Sir Thomas was a member of the House of Commons— the pro-slavery lobby had lost its sway. If Austen's sole interest in having Sir Thomas travel to Antigua were, say, to get him offstage so his children could get into trouble without his interference, she could just as easily have dispatched him to some other family property anywhere else in England. But Austen carefully, if quietly, designates Sir Thomas as a slaveholder—even having him travel to Antigua via Liverpool, famous specifically as a slave-trading port—precisely to raise questions about his moral authority—both as a father and as a national figure. In doing so, she underscores a moral point that was no longer either obscure or controversial at the time, i.e., that slaveholding is a form of misrule that has disastrous consequences under a man's own roof. Neither at home nor abroad is Sir Thomas a responsible figure of authority. Novel and movie alike are at pains to dramatize the moral effect of bad education, and both lay the faults of waywardness and weakness, so evident in their children, at the door of parents whose ideas about education, and whose personal examples, are lacking.

In a climactic scene of Rozema's invention, Fanny discovers a series of sketches depicting the torture and rape of Sir Thomas's slaves. Once again aware of an obligation to balance creative invention with historical accuracy, Rozema here uses sketches by and based on Austen's contemporary William Blake. These are not the kinds of pictures we usually associate with Jane Austen, however, and on their account the movie almost got an R-rating. Needless to say, the sketches are supposed to be shocking, and on this score, Rozema's methods differ from Austen's. Preferring indirection, understatement, hints, and gleaning, Austen would probably demur from the dramatic effect Rozema creates in the movie, but like most writers at the time, she would concur in the moral. Sir Thomas's failures of moral authority abroad lead to his moral turpitude at home. He has been depraved by the unchecked power slaveholding and trading illegitimately confers upon him, and as a result he makes no attempt even to appear right-thinking or dignified. Thus we see him nastily savoring racist drivel found in Edward Long's *History of Jamaica* (1774), volumes Austen almost certainly knew. Similarly, by casting Lindsay Duncan as both Mrs. Price and Lady Bertram, temperamentally similar sisters separated by the gulf of class, Rozema intensifies the stupor of native apathy by supplying Lady Bertram with laudanum to boot. Rozema foregrounds and augments the unseemliness present throughout the novel, and only at the end of the film does she let up.

If Rozema is careful to bring out the historic moral and social issues underpinning Austen's novel, she is just as imaginative and resourceful about finding a cinematic way to offer what many of us love about Austen in the first place, what other movies never deliver: Austen's presence as a narrator. Rozema accomplishes this fidelity by unapologetic innovation in another respect. Instead of the dutiful, self-denying, inhibited, and frail girl of the novel—Fanny cannot ride a pony or trim the roses without extreme fatigue—Rozema's

Fanny Price is sturdy, self-possessed (if shy), plucky, and physically energetic. Generations of readers have been sharply and passionately divided on the Fanny question. Library shelves and chat rooms are teeming with debates about whether it is or is not possible actually to *like* Fanny. In her very abjection, Austen's heroine strikes me, at least, as a fascinating and unprecedented character. It was surprising to encounter Rozema's change, and at first a bit hard to stop regretting it. But once I did, I found her innovations astute and rewarding, accomplishing what we might not expect from Austen adaptations nowadays: a sense of freshness and even of surprise. Clearly, the novelistic techniques that give us so much access to the diffident Fanny's inwardness in the novel simply cannot be translated to cinematic representation. And so, to render Fanny at all Rozema hit upon a stratagem that conduces at one and the same time to the faithfulness and to the originality of her film: she makes Fanny into the teller of her tale.

In Rozema's movie, Fanny, likeably played by Frances O'Connor, retreats to her room not to struggle with feelings of injury that she can scarcely permit herself to feel much less to articulate, but to engage in the sweetest revenge of all, writing well. Fanny scribbles the raucous stories Austen wrote when she was a girl—"Henry and Eliza," for example, where the heroine finds herself imprisoned, her two fingers bitten off and devoured by her hungry children; and "The History of England," where Fanny (thinking of her snooty relations?) observes of the row Joan of Arc caused among the English, "They should not have burnt her but they did." Readers who know and love Austen's uproarious and irreverent early work will no doubt recognize how widely Rozema has ranged in order to provide Fanny with choice quips, and will probably enjoy making their own list of favorites. Mine include "I often think it odd that History should be so dull, for a great deal of it must be invention" from *Northanger Abbey;* or "Sophia shrieked and fainted and I screamed and instantly ran mad" from *Love and Friendship.* Devoted readers of Austen's letters will also recognize the lines "I am a wild beast," "Brush your hair, but not all off," and the plangent "I see more distinctly through the rain." By weaving so much of Austen's own prose into the screenplay, Rozema transforms Fanny's voice into a version of Austen's, and conveys a story in a manner that is decidedly less staid and precious than what some audiences expect from Austen. In the process, of course, Rozema also gets across the novel's humor—no small feat—for as a writing-heroine, Fanny takes over the narrator's acerbic lines, as when she says that Maria was "prepared for matrimony by a hatred of home, by the misery of disappointed affection and contempt of the man she was to marry" or describes her wedding with "her mother stood with salts in her hand, expecting to be agitated, and her aunt tried to cry." Rozema has ranged wide and deep among Austen's letters, novels, youthful sketches (the "journals" referred to in the credits) and integrated their prose into her screenplay.

Rozema's movie is also compelling in its evocations of sexuality. On this subject, some readers, viewers, and reviewers have been apt to sound priggish. Having assumed that the spinsterly Austen was too prim and proper ever to think about much less to write about sex, such readers suggest that it is somehow indecent, gratuitous, and just plain wrong to portray sexuality in Austen's novels, and so refuse to recognize the sexuality that is very clearly there as sexuality at all. The demonstrable facts are that Austen was clear-sighted and unsentimental about sex, and that *Mansfield Park* is particularly suffused with frustrated, illicit, wayward, or polymorphous sexuality. *Pride and Prejudice* may be straightforward and at best euphoric on the subject of sexuality, but *Mansfield Park* describes a world that is not healthy in any respect, and in sexuality least of all. In the novel, hero Edmund inadvertently tortures heroine Fanny by reporting how he and his father discussed her improved "figure"—referring no doubt to the sexual maturation that has occurred while Sir Thomas was abroad—while Fanny's alcoholic father, noting the same maturation, refers to her only "to make her the object of a coarse joke." The novel's crisis hinges on a case of adultery that to Fanny's mind—if not to Austen's, which is imperturbable on the subject—seems luridly rank. And when Fanny's father reads about his niece's disgrace in the newspaper, he swears "by G—if she belonged to me, I'd give her the rope's end as long as I could stand over her," a statement certainly not without erotic resonance, and which strongly suggests the context of slavery debates, where the sick brutality of such scenes were often invoked. In the novel, even licit love teeters on an incestuousness: rakish Henry gets turned on to Fanny by watching her complexion glow in the presence of her brother William (who is not in the movie version), and Edmund greets Fanny (his childhood playmate, and the woman he will soon marry) as his "only sister." Nor is homoerotic badinage off limits, for bad-girl Mary does indeed flirt with Edmund by rehearsing with Fanny, and the narrator describes the spell Mary casts over Fanny as a "fascination," a term that carries an erotic charge. Far from sullying the pristine Austen with the unwholesomeness of modern sexualities, Rozema's movie actually condenses and downplays much of the novel's interest to explore unseemly aspects of the subject.

For the sake of economy and consolidation, Rozema's movie does indeed depart from the novel, but on the score of sexuality she invents little. In the climactic scene, where Fanny actually discovers Maria's and Henry's adultery, Rozema briefly shows it in the raw as Austen of course does not, preferring reportage to direct presentation, but this scene certainly feels as unseemly and as disgraceful as Austen would wish it to be. And when Rozema evokes sexuality in its subtler forms—as a sort of yearning or self-discovery—she is faithful and evocative. Ballroom scenes, for example, are standard fare in Austen movies, and often they've become starchy productions in which one senses the presence of dance coaches and etiquette advisors off-camera, hectoring actors into the appearance of historically correct merriment. But the ball here is not shot as a set-piece of Regency spectacle. At times, it is conceived almost as a semi-private scene so as to bring out Fanny's awakening to the pleasure of her body and the circulation of erotic interest between and among the two principal couples. In the novel as well as the movie, Fanny is thrilled and also confused by these new pleasures. In a telling scene in the movie, she stands by her attic window after the ball is over, and as she spies her admirer Henry looking up and bowing gallantly, she composes. "Run mad as often as you choose," she whispers, snuffing out the candle so she cannot be seen from below, "but do not faint."

Clearly, unlike her characters in *Love and Friendship*, this Fanny is determined not to lose her head, but her very determination tells us how easily she might. She carries a torch for her earnest but dim cousin Edmund. But while *his* touch alone is enough to take poor Fanny's breath away, he seems smitten by Henry's kinky, amoral, and trite sister Mary, and as a result Fanny is vulnerable to Henry's attentions. Passion here as in the novel is mobile and bewildering. It is not the easy and tidy stuff of Harlequin romances. In a daring and clever move, Rozema grafts onto her screenplay the Bigg-Wither episode of Austen's own life, in which Austen received and accepted a proposal which would have made her the mistress of a large estate and enabled her to provide for her parents and her beloved sister, and to assist the careers of her brothers, but changed her mind over the course of the night and retracted her acceptance the next morning. Like Austen herself, Rozema's Fanny finally accepts Henry's proposal, only to recant the next morning. This is an inspired touch since the novel allows that Fanny would indeed have said "yes" to

Henry *after* Edmund's marriage to Mary. The effect of Rozema's adaptation is to bring Fanny more clearly under the influence of the moral and erotic confusion elsewhere, without sacrificing our respect for the courage she shows in resisting her uncle's mercenary bullying, or our sympathy for her patient struggle to do and feel as she ought.

Rozema's other movies (*I've Heard the Mermaids Singing, When Night is Falling*) are distinctive for their mix of the sublime and the amiable. Like them, *Mansfield Park* is about vision and flight, about creativity itself. The movie opens with dizzying shots of paper, paper seen so close up as to appear utterly unrecognizable. It's an evocative shot because it immediately brings forward the question that is central to Austen's art and to the love of Austen's art: scale. How can an author whose view of the world was so "limited," the question runs, possibly be considered so powerful, so great? The answer is in Rozema's understated opening even supposedly limited material, looked at attentively and with the eyes of genius, can be infinite—just as the leaves of paper seem to evoke the English fields over which the camera will later fly so ecstatically. Gradually, we hear a girl's voice and then voices of hundreds of girls, and as these cream-colored sheets fall, we finally recognize them as pages of a manuscript; pages as mobile and vital as the dancers we later see at the ball. Rozema's *Mansfield Park* is about getting free, about the liberating rewards of patience and intelligence we see in Fanny, but also about the expansive, uplifting, and liberating clarity Austen's own art gives us.

" 'I can't get out, I can't get out ,' the starling says." Rozema uses Austen's allusion to a caged bird in Laurence Sterne's famous *Sentimental Journey* to protest the confinement—of slaves, of women, and of talents. Taking her cue from Austen's famous lines "Let other pens dwell on guilt and misery. I quit such odious subjects as soon as I can," Rozema lingers over swarms of starlings taking wing outdoors, and her camera soars rapturously and rapidly over the hillside. These are thrilling moments, as Fanny narrates a fittingly accelerated conclusion in which most of the characters get off relatively easy, even if they never really do get free: the wicked (Mrs. Norris, Maria) are confined to the hell of each other's company in a remote cottage; the rakish Crawfords return to fashionable life in London, fettered by their worldliness; and the chastened Sir Thomas, reforming his ways as much as he can, grows tobacco instead of sugar! "It could have turned out differently, I suppose," Fanny says repeatedly over scenes that freeze the action and break the illusion of realism to call attention to the benign yet unblinking intervention of her art. Fanny happily gets her man, of course, but our happiness comes from knowing that in becoming the author of *Mansfield Park* she is the one who has really gotten out at last.

Perhaps Austen could have predicted how aptly her remark "One half of the world cannot understand the pleasures of the other" would describe her own fans. Some readers have always preferred to think of Austen as a serene, domestic, and placid writer whose work studiously excludes the disruptive, the passionate, the complicated. But others have loved her for very different qualities—for the energy, the irreverence, and the wicked sharpness of her wit, for the keenness of her social commentary on a world where morals and manners are often at odds, and for the power of her characters' passions, passions sharpened by intelligence and complicated by good manners. Rozema's *Mansfield Park* best captures why my half of the world loves Austen.

Finally a director has taken real risks and reaped real rewards with her work, treating her novels not as a museum piece or as a sacred text but as a living presence whose power inspires flight. *Mansfield Park* is an audacious and perceptive cinematic evocation of Austen's distinctively sharp yet forgiving vision.

—Claudia L. Johnson

1   INT. CREDITS SEQUENCE

CREDITS appear over extreme close-ups of thousands of very tiny words written in ink on old letter paper and "crossed" on the page (letters were sometimes written both horizontally & vertically and even diagonally on the same page to save postage & paper).

SFX: Sound of whispering. One girl's voice, overdubbed, briefly sounds like a thousand voices.

MUSIC: early music string quartet with distant African drums.

END CREDITS

2   INT. PORTSMOUTH BEDROOM—DAWN—PORTSMOUTH, ENGLAND, 1796

Silence. An eleven-year-old FANNY PRICE and her eight-year-old sister, SUSAN, lie curled up in "spoons" in bed like two dark kittens. Fanny is whispering to her sister.

> YOUNG FANNY
> (dramatic whisper)
> . . . and just as Eliza was majestically removing a fifty-pound bank note from the drawer to her own purse, we were suddenly, most impertinently interrupted by old MacDonald himself. We called up all the winning dignity of our sex to do what must be done: Sophia shrieked and fainted and I screamed and instantly ran mad. For an hour and a quarter did we continue in this unfortunate situation—Sophia fainting every moment and I running mad as often.

Little Susan can't help chuckling. Fanny sits up in the bed to aid the delivery of her tale. (Her eyeline is very close to camera.)

> YOUNG FANNY
> Finally, we regained our senses, escaped and hastened to

London. And as soon as we had happily disencumbered ourselves from the weight of so much money, we began to think of returning to our mothers, but accidentally heard that they had both starved to death. . . .

> MRS. PRICE (VOICE-OVER)
> (angry)

FANNY!

SFX: *Loud footsteps approach.*

> YOUNG FANNY
> (whispered)

Good-bye, Susy.

Susan hugs her urgently.

> SUSAN

Think of lots of good stories for me and eat thousands of tarts.

> YOUNG FANNY
> (mock stern)

And you, little girl, continue to brush your hair but not all off.

They both smile. Enter MRS. PRICE, a haggard, worried woman.

> MRS. PRICE

Fanny, he's here.

Reveal a crowded, dirty little room—half-eaten food on the floor, bugs, filthy clothes. There are three little sleeping boys in another bed in the same room.

> MRS. PRICE

Wake up, say good-bye to your sister.

3 EXT. PORTSMOUTH HOUSE—DAWN—CONTINUOUS

The chaise stands outside the grimy row house. Two of the three boys from her room stumble outside to join Susan and the four other children who wait to wave her off.

> MRS. PRICE
>
> Sorry for the delay.

> CARRIAGE DRIVER
>
> Just hurry, then.

Mrs. Price hugs Fanny, which seems to surprise her. Fanny tries to extend the hug a bit longer but her mother won't let her.

Fanny steps into the chaise. Her mother throws a marine sack and her collection of books and papers in behind her.

The carriage pulls away. Fanny waves good-bye.

> YOUNG FANNY
>
> Good-bye everyone.

> EVERYONE
>
> 'Bye Fan. 'Bye Sis. See you. You look fabulous. Toodleloo, you lucky cow.

> YOUNG FANNY
>
> Good-bye Mama.

> MRS. PRICE
>
> Give my regards to my sisters.

The carriage pulls away.

Yes, Mama. And you will write to tell me when I'm to
return?

Mrs. Price half nods, half waves as she turns away.

4   EXT. PORTSMOUTH STREETS—DAWN—CONTINUOUS

*The carriage rattles through the poorest streets of the harbor town. Seagulls cry.
Very bumpy ride.*

4A   INT. PORTSMOUTH HOUSE—DAWN—MOMENTS LATER

*Mrs. Price stands at the counter chopping a withered carrot. Her children return to
their beds. The handle on the knife she is chopping with breaks and she bursts into
tears.*

5   EXT. CLIFF OVERLOOKING HARBOR—DAWN—MOMENTS LATER

*Inside the carriage, the rattle and shake up the hill is deafening. Fanny rides away
from Portsmouth.*

*Suddenly Fanny's carriage stops. Fanny puts her head out of the window. The
carriage driver adjusts a strap on one of his horses.*

*Fanny looks back out at the harbor through the mist on the sea. She hears waves
on the beach, then what sounds like a low mournful tone, then more. Gradually,
through the mist, she hears the saddest African ballad ever.*

YOUNG FANNY

Do you hear that?

The carriage driver listens.

CARRIAGE DRIVER

Black cargo, miss.

YOUNG FANNY

Black cargo?

CARRIAGE DRIVER

Yea. Slaves. Probably some captain or heroic ship doctor
brought home a few darkies as gifts for the wife.

The mist covers the boat again. Fanny strains to hear more, but the carriage jerks
into motion.

5   INT. CARRIAGE—DAWN—CONTINUOUS

Loud carriage noise again. Fanny tries to absorb the carriage driver's information.

7   EXT. COUNTRYSIDE—EARLY, MID AND
LATE DAY

High floating bird's-eye view shots of the carriage.

8   INT. CARRIAGE—NIGHT

Fanny tries to sleep but can't.

9 EXT. NORTHAMPTON ROAD AND MANSFIELD PARK—NIGHT

In the darkness Fanny perceives the carriage passing through a pair of iron gates, along a tree-lined path, and into the forecourt of Mansfield Park—then through another gateway into the inner courtyard. The place seems immense.

Fanny climbs out exhausted. She stumbles and almost falls on the ground. Through Fanny's eyes the place has a vaguely sinister, decadent air.

The carriage driver bangs on the door, no answer.

CARRIAGE DRIVER
(yelling)
Mrs. Norris. Hello?! Hello, Mrs. Norris?

No answer. Finally, an expensively dressed but severely disheveled 17-year-old, TOM, leans out of one of the windows.

TOM
(slight slur)
It's five o'clock in the morning.

CARRIAGE DRIVER
A "Mrs. Norris" arranged to have this girl brought here. It's her niece or something.

TOM
Mrs. Norris lives in the parsonage over there.

Tom leans/falls back into the room.

CARRIAGE DRIVER
Can you fetch her?

TOM (OFFSCREEN)
I don't fetch. Where's Baddeley anyway?

CARRIAGE DRIVER

But I was told most definitely to drop her at the front
entrance of Mansfield Park.

TOM (OFFSCREEN)

Then drop her!

The driver looks at Fanny, then at the parsonage.

CARRIAGE DRIVER
(to Fanny)

Just stay here. I'll get Mrs. Norris.

YOUNG FANNY

Thank you.

*He drives off. Fanny is left standing at the front door with her marine sack at her
feet. It's quite chilly.*

10 EXT. MANSFIELD PARK FRONT STEPS—
DAWN—ONE HOUR LATER

*MRS. NORRIS hurries in through the inner court, huffing and puffing to great effect.
She's a busy woman and she likes people to know it.*

YOUNG FANNY
You must be my aunt, Aunt Norris?

MRS. NORRIS

Yes. Yes. He brought you *two hours* too early! Come in.
Come in.

Mrs. Norris hurries into the house, leading Fanny in by the arm.

11 INT. ENTRANCE HALL—MANSFIELD PARK—DAWN—CONTINUOUS

Fanny looks in awe at the spacious hall paved with stone. Their voices echo.

MRS. NORRIS

Now, let us have a look at you.

Mrs. Norris checks Fanny over. In this new context she looks especially ragged and thin.

MRS. NORRIS (CONT'D)

Well, I'm sure you have many other qualities. Is that all you
brought with you? (*Fanny nods*) I had no idea it had got so
bad. (*to servant*) Ellis, gather up the children. Sir Thomas,
she's here! Our new little charge.

SIR THOMAS BERTRAM enters the entrance hall, smoothing his hair. He is stern and reserved even when he's trying to be friendly.

SIR THOMAS

Hello Fanny.

YOUNG FANNY

Hello, Sir Thomas. Greetings from my family, sir.

SIR THOMAS

Yes, thank you. How was your journey?

YOUNG FANNY

Lovely, sir. I had no idea England was so big.

SIR THOMAS

But you came, what, a hundred miles . . . ?

Mrs. Norris smiles. ELLIS enters and whispers to Mrs. Norris.

YOUNG FANNY

Yes, sir. Impressive.

SIR THOMAS

Indeed it is. Well then . . .

MRS. NORRIS

Sir Thomas: Tom says he's ill and as you know, Edmund isn't
back from Eton until later today. The girls should be with us
in a moment.

SIR THOMAS

Thank you, Mrs. Norris. Then, why don't you get her
settled in with yourself and Mr. Norris at the parsonage,
and we'll do the introductions of the children later.

MRS. NORRIS
(prepared surprise)

With Mr. Norris and myself?!

SIR THOMAS

Yes, I thought . . .

Mrs. Norris shakes her head.

MRS. NORRIS

Oh. Oh. Oh, no, no. There's been a misunderstanding, sir.
When I suggested we take in Lady Bertram's and my poor
niece, I wouldn't have . . .

YOUNG FANNY

Please do not trouble yourselves on my behalf, I can just . . .

MRS. NORRIS

Shhh. You speak when you are spoken to.

SIR THOMAS

(embarrassed for Fanny)

Excuse us—um—Miss Price.

Fanny doesn't realize she's been dismissed, so Mrs. Norris takes her arm and leads her through the entrance hall to the anteroom. On her way we reveal a beautiful woman sleeping in a chair in front of a smouldering fire. She's holding a wheezing PUG on her lap. This is the vague, contented being known as LADY BERTRAM.

11   INT. ANTEROOM/GREAT STAIRCASE— MORNING

Mrs. Norris deposits Fanny outside the great hall and closes the door.

Cut to a pair of handsome, almost identical blonde girls of thirteen and twelve years old at the top of the stairs, MARIA and JULIA. They are old for their age and strive to be older still. Maria has the edge in confidence and beauty. Julia is forever trying to catch up. They look at Fanny.

JULIA

Maybe she'll like to play Old Maid.

MARIA

(whispering)

Or, at the very least, be one.

Julia giggles. The girls descend the stairs grandly. Fanny nods politely. Maria and Julia curtsy. Fanny does some kind of bow/curtsylike thing.

MARIA (CONT'D)

Good morning. I am Maria Elizabeth Bertram.

JULIA

And I am Julia Frances Bertram. Pleased to make your acquaintance.

YOUNG FANNY

Pleased to meet you.

No subjects rush to mind. Maria curtsies and leads Julia towards the great hall, leaving the doors slightly ajar. Fanny can hear.

MRS. NORRIS (OFFSCREEN)

With all my faults you know I have a warm heart: and, poor as I am, would rather deny myself the necessaries of life than do an ungenerous thing. . . . It's just that Mr. Norris could no more tolerate the noise of a child than he could fly. . . .

Camera slowly circles Fanny as she tries to comprehend.

13 INT. GREAT HALL—MORNING—CONTINUOUS

SIR THOMAS

But . . . (*meaningfully*) *cousins in love* et cetera . . . It might not be wise to have her here in the house with . . . the boys . . .

MRS. NORRIS

My dear Sir Thomas: but of all things upon earth *that* is least likely to happen; if you breed her up with them from this time, and suppose her even to have the beauty of an angel, and she will never be more to either than a sister.

14 INT. ANTEROOM—MORNING—CONTINUOUS

Fanny seems perplexed. SFX: The pug barks.

> SIR THOMAS (OFFSCREEN)
> I suppose there is truth to that. . . .

15 INT. GREAT HALL—MORNING—CONTINUOUS

Sir Thomas addresses Maria and Julia.

> SIR THOMAS
> Well then, it is settled. Maria, Julia . . . listen. We must
> prepare ourselves for gross ignorance, some meanness of
> opinions, and a very distressing vulgarity of manner.

16 INT. ANTE ROOM—MORNING—CONTINUOUS

Hearing this, Fanny smoothes her dress self-consciously.

> MRS. NORRIS (OFFSCREEN)
> These are not incurable faults.

INT. GREAT HALL—MORNING—CONTINUOUS

Lady Bertram has woken.

> LADY BERTRAM
> I hope she will not tease my poor pug, I have but just got
> Julia to leave him alone.

SIR THOMAS

Of course, darling.

MRS. NORRIS

I will train her up properly, sister. Though I can't image her
ever being as lovely as our Maria and Julia.

SIR THOMAS
(to girls)

But you girls must never be arrogant towards her.

MRS. NORRIS

It is unbecoming.

SIR THOMAS

Your rank, fortune, rights, and expectations will always be
different. She is not your equal. But that should not be
apparent to her. It is a point of great delicacy.

MRS. NORRIS

Yes, very delicate, yes.

18   INT. VARIOUS ROOMS (LIBRARY, STUDY,
BILLIARD ROOM, CONSERVATORY, KITCHEN,
SERVANT CHAMBERS AND CORRIDOR. MARIA'S
FRILLY BEDROOM, TOM'S BEDROOM—DAY

*Mrs. Norris leads Fanny through the house at breakneck speed. (Jump cut jagged
handheld shots.) Overload of images. Intercut with Fanny's face.*

*Seen in full daylight, all aspects of Mansfield Park have a faded, run-down quality,
like a great beauty who is short on both hope and means.*

MRS. NORRIS

That's the great hall of course, this is the anteroom, the

dining parlor in there. And over there . . . the conservatory.
I hope you don't tend towards sulkiness, dear.

We catch a glimpse of a family of servants sitting together having tea and playing with their child.

                    MRS. NORRIS (CONT'D)
That way to the cellar. Your mother certainly had the
inclination—clearly marrying to *disoblige* her family. The
billiard room, for the men of course. Remember there is
moderation in all things.

She partially opens the sliding doors that reveal Sir Thomas's study. Dark, mysterious room.

                    MRS. NORRIS (CONT'D)
And here is Sir Thomas's study. *Never* disturb him here. He
is weighed-down with great cares at this moment. (*with
some reverence*) This is his personal sanctuary.

Fanny looks through an open door to see a long hallway with almost no roof. Some rubble falls.

                    MRS. NORRIS CONT'D
Oh, that's the west wing, soon to be repaired, if Tom could
set aside his horses and the dice for long enough.

They arrive at the top of the stairs onto the second floor.

                    MRS. NORRIS (CONT'D)
Sir Thomas's extraordinary library. Lady Bertram enjoys
napping here most afternoons. (*whispering*) She never really
recovered from the birth of Julia, you know. She is quite
dependent on me.

Fanny nods as she stops to look at an unusually large portrait of Tom. In the painting, he holds up a brush to a canvas. A skeleton stands behind him with its hand on his shoulder.

MRS. NORRIS
(disapproving)
Yes, yes, Tom did it of himself. Very modern, very modern.

19 INT. STAIRWELL & HALLWAY—DAY— CONTINUOUS

They mount a set of stairs up to the third floor. Fanny is smiling bravely.

MRS. NORRIS
And up here, come quick now, (huffing and puffing) the maids' rooms and the manservant's rooms down there. You will be *my assistant,* you understand.

And what was formerly the nursery and then the governess's room and is now . . . your very own room.

20 INT. FANNY'S ROOM—DAY—CONTINUOUS

Fanny looks into a fairly large but low-ceilinged attic room littered with dust-covered junk. A dormer window looks out onto the garden. On one side, a mean little bed.

YOUNG FANNY
Excuse me but . . .

MRS. NORRIS
Yes?

YOUNG FANNY
How long am I expected to remain here?

MRS. NORRIS
Well, that depends, doesn't it? (smiling) But if all goes well, forever.

Fanny stands, stunned, in the middle of her room. Mrs. Norris leaves.

YOUNG FANNY (VOICE-OVER)

Dear Susy: Despite the incomprehensible luxury of the place . . .

Fanny looks to camera:

. . . I can augur nothing but misery from all I have seen at Mansfield Park.

Fanny turns around in her room trying to hold herself together but suddenly loses heart: She sits herself down on floor and sobs.

An earnest 13-year-old boy walks towards Fanny's door. This is EDMUND, who loves to think himself a philosopher and has no idea how good-looking he is. He stops when he sees her crying and watches for a moment through the open door. Something in her woundedness stirs him, his eyes brim with sympathy.

Fanny looks up. Suddenly aware that he is spying on her, he debates with himself as to whether he should leave or say something. Embarrassed, he steps out of sight. Fanny looks up again to see him step into the room with his glasses upside down on his head.

She can't help but smile. She tries to hide the fact of her tears.

EDMUND

Don't worry, I'm all for crying, crying is good. It makes your hair grow. And you are good at it.

YOUNG FANNY

Don't make fun of me.

EDMUND

I'm not, I'm not . . . (*his glasses fall*) I'm writing an essay on stupidity, you see. I expect to publish it in my magazine at Eton, *The Loiterer.*

He puts them back on his face.

EDMUND (CONT'D)

Is it working?

YOUNG FANNY

Is what working?

EDMUND

My behavior, is it making you feel better?

His smile is irresistible.

YOUNG FANNY

It's certainly distracting.

EDMUND

So it is working. Right then. Then let me introduce myself: I'm Edmund Bertram, your cousin. You know we're really not as terrible as we might appear here at Mansfield Park. . . . in fact I have it on very reliable authority that we are worse. . . .

YOUNG FANNY

Not possible.

21   EXT. HALLWAY—DAY—CONTINUOUS

EDMUND (CONT'D)

Possible. (*sitting down*) So tell me, who do you miss and why?

YOUNG FANNY (VOICE-OVER)

I told Edmund about you especially, Susy.

Camera pulls away down hallway.

DISSOLVE TO:

22 INT. DRAWING ROOM—LATER SAME DAY

Fanny admires Edmund as he prepares the paper for her.

> YOUNG FANNY (VOICE-OVER)
> He asked me if I wished to write to you and I said I had no
> paper. And didn't he gave me enough for more letters and
> stories than you shall ever want to receive.

*Loving details: "mending" the quill with a penknife, ruling lines, sprinkling powder on
the paper, etc.*

23 INT. FANNY'S ROOM—NIGHT—AN HOUR LATER

*Fanny sits at her desk with another large stack of paper beside her. Fanny looks into
the lens.*

> YOUNG FANNY (TO CAMERA)
> By the way, Eliza eloped to Paris with her lover.
> Unfortunately she lived beyond her means and was
> imprisoned and partially eaten by her two young sons. But
> she intends to murder the guards. I'll keep you abreast of
> any developments.

24 INT. PORTSMOUTH CHILDHOOD BEDROOM—DAY

Susan is reading a letter from Fanny.

> YOUNG FANNY/SUSAN (VOICE-OVER)
> P.S. Could you please assure mother that I am improving
> myself daily.

Fanny sits at her desk in her tiny room with her pen in hand.

> YOUNG FANNY
>
> The History of England. Henry the Sixth.

(Audio note: Voices of Young Fanny and Older Fanny overlap, gradually maturing.)

She looks into camera.

> YOUNG FANNY A. (TO CAMERA)
>
> It was in this reign that Joan of Arc lived and made such a row among the English. They should not have burnt her but they did. . . .

DISSOLVE TO: Fanny, a little older, her hair is longer.

> YOUNG FANNY B. (TO CAMERA)
>
> Henry the seventh. His Majesty died, and was succeeded by his son Henry whose only merit was his not being quite so bad as his daughter Elizabeth.

DISSOLVE TO: Fanny, older (different actress). She stands up and walks away from us toward her window. She is now less a little girl and more a young woman.

OLDER FANNY C.

Henry the eighth. I'll save you the task of telling what you've already heard, and myself of recounting what I do not perfectly recollect.

DISSOLVE TO: *Fanny. She turns and looks into the lens. She is now about twenty-one years old (our main actress).*

FANNY PRICE (TO CAMERA)

And then that disgrace to humanity, that pest of society, Elizabeth, who, murderess and wicked queen that she was, confined her cousin, the lovely Mary Queen of Scots for *NINETEEN YEARS* and then brought her to an untimely, unmerited, and scandalous death. Much to the eternal shame of the monarchy and the entire kingdom.

Pull back to reveal Edmund (now 26), totally surprised and delighted. He picks up the paper Fanny is reading. We read the title: THE HISTORY OF ENGLAND.

EDMUND

(reading)

"By a partial, prejudiced, and ignorant historian." Fanny, you are awful.

Fanny thrives on his amusement.

FANNY

All those quarrels and wars. The men all good for nothing, and hardly any women at all—it is very tiresome. I often think it odd that history should be so dull, for a great deal of it must be invention.

EDMUND

You are a great invention. I shall have to bend your supple mind in more strict a fashion. I think the situation calls for some . . . *(smile)* . . . Shakespeare.

Fanny almost gasps with delight at the suggestion. She leaps up and runs out of the room. Edmund is soon after her.

26 INT. SIR THOMAS'S STUDY—AFTERNOON—CONTINUOUS

Sir Thomas stares in disbelief at a ledger page full of figures. Through his open door we see Fanny slide down the banister. Edmund races ahead. She laughs out loud.

> SIR THOMAS
> (irritated)
> Fanny Price, could you at least try to act with some
> decorum.

27 EXT. STABLES—AFTERNOON—MOMENTS LATER

They run into the stable hand in hand.

27A INT. ANTEROOM AND 1ST-FLOOR STAIRWELL—AFTERNOON

Sir Thomas and Mrs. Norris watch through different windows with a distinct air of disapproval. Edmund notices them at the window. Fanny sees their disapproval as well.

28 EXT. FIELD—AFTERNOON—MOMENTS LATER

The two of them ride full gallop. Edmund rides splendidly. Fanny, riding side saddle, bounces about a bit much but the spirit is willing. Slow motion on their flushed cheeks, on Edmund's thighs gripping the horse, on the horse's nostrils, on the wind in the trees.

29 EXT. WOODS—AFTERNOON—AN HOUR LATER

They enter the wood. The sweating horses slow to a trot and finally a walk. Both are out of breath. Edmund steals an appreciative glance at Fanny.

> FANNY

What?

> EDMUND

That leap was not without spectacle, Fanny.

> FANNY
> (patting her mare's neck)

It was Mrs. Shakespeare who did the leaping.

> EDMUND

So you like her?

> FANNY

Like her? She is my sanity and my refuge, Edmund, I can't thank you enough for giving her to me.

> EDMUND

My gifts are nothing compared to yours, Fanny. My writing is wood next to your wild constructions.

> FANNY
> (mock dramatic)

Oh yes, I am a wild beast. I'm sure Sir Thomas would agree.

> EDMUND

Don't concern yourself with his gravity, Fanny, he . . . has many things to preoccupy him.

Beat.

FANNY

Like?

EDMUND

Like . . . he bought a shipload of men and a few women from
Loanga, West Africa. They work our sugar plantation in
Antigua. And they are unhappy at the moment, the
abolitionists are making inroads and . . .

FANNY

And they must miss their families, they must be furious.
Wouldn't you be?

EDMUND

Oh, yes, terribly. Their misery seems to require more than
a few weighty sighs, but . . . at the same time Mansfield Park
is entirely dependent on the profits of that operation. . . .
It's not, it's not . . . clear.

29A INT. STUDY/''DOG ROOM''/UPSTAIRS HALLWAY

Sir Thomas charges after Tom. Both are enraged.

SIR THOMAS

You will do as I say!

TOM

And become like you? Even I have principles.

We see Fanny looking on from the corner.

30   INT. "DOG ROOM"—DAY

*We see Fanny carrying a tray with a distinctly medicinal-looking blue glass bottle
past Sir Thomas's study, which Sir Thomas and Tom just left. She deposits the tray
beside Lady Bertram, who quickly sets about putting her drops of laudanum into her
glass.*

> LADY BERTRAM
>
> Ah, you are an angel.

*Fanny stops to look at a LITHOGRAPH on the wall: It shows a proud white man in
an Antiguan sugar cane field surrounded by happy slaves. We hear more yelling.*

> FANNY (VOICE-OVER)
>
> Dear Susy: News items: Sir Thomas has dragged Tom along
> with him to the West Indies to "protect our interests
> there."

31   EXT. SOTHERTON—DAY

CU on Maria walking (right to left) smiling broadly.

> FANNY (VOICE-OVER)
>
> Maria has found herself a fiancé, a Mr. Rushworth, with
> whom everyone is quite delighted. . . .

Pan over to the magnificent though vaguely prisonlike estate of SOTHERTON.

> FANNY AND EDMUND (VOICE-OVER)
>
> . . . except Edmund, who says that (*add EDMUND VO:*) "if
> he had not twelve thousand pounds a year we would think
> him prodigiously dim."

*Continue pan to MR. RUSHWORTH, a not-too-swift-looking young man following
behind while clearing something out of his ear.*

*Continue pan to a less-than-overjoyed Julia, who trudges along behind Rushworth
and Maria.*

FANNY (VOICE-OVER)

Consequently, there is a new urgency to Julia's search for a suitor.

32 INT. FANNY'S ROOM—DAY

FANNY (TO CAMERA)

And Mrs. Norris's husband died . . .

33 INT. PARSONAGE—DAY

Shot of a man's head sinking into his soup.

33I INT. FANNY'S ROOM—DAY

FANNY (CONT'D)

. . . which did not seem to inconvenience her very much at all. She has moved into Mansfield proper, where life is decidedly less expensive for her. What joy is mine.

Camera looks out of her window toward the parsonage.

34 EXT. PARSONAGE—DAY—A MONTH LATER

A fleshy, 45-year-old parson and his overdressed wife move their furniture into the parsonage.

FANNY (VOICE-OVER)

So there is a new clergyman moved into the parsonage.

35 INT. FANNY'S ROOM—DAY

Fanny stands at her window looking out. She sighs.

FANNY (CONT'D)

And . . . life seems nothing more than a quick succession of
busy nothings.

36 INT. GREAT HALL—NEXT DAY

*Maria and Julia are playing cards lackadaisically. Fanny is reading but flips through
her pages. Edmund is tending the fire. Rushworth is draped over the chaise longue
with a cloth over his eyes. Time seems to pass heavily.*

*Lady Bertram snoozes contentedly, the bottle of laudanum beside her. Mrs. Norris
stands at the door.*

MRS. NORRIS

They are half brother and sister to the new parson's wife. I
expect you to entertain them with suitable attention and
animation . . . (*no reaction*) not to mention alacrity.

*Clearly no one is in the mood for obligatory socializing. We hear Baddeley letting the
guests in.*

RUSHWORTH

I might need the morning to recover from the Withrow's
ball last night, Mrs. Norris. I'm just a mite . . . sluggish.

MARIA

Indeed.

MRS. NORRIS

Mr. Rushworth, if you please.

Mr. Rushworth sits up.

The door opens. Everyone looks. Stillness. The room brightens just slightly as if there's a surge in the voltage of the air. A ever-so-slight breeze enters the room with the CRAWFORDS.

MRS. NORRIS
May I introduce Mary Crawford.

MARY CRAWFORD has an expensive beauty. Her fine, dark eyes rest in a look that manages mischief without childishness. Her entirely black, almost form-fitting dress cuts a silhouette of drama. She looks over the room approvingly, engaging each person in direct eye contact. Fanny, unused to such intense acknowledgment, looks away. Edmund drinks her in.

MRS. NORRIS (CONT'D)
And her brother, Henry Crawford.

HENRY CRAWFORD, standing beside Mary, is proud and very quick. He resembles his sister. His laughing look captures the attention of everyone in the room, especially that of Julia and Maria.

Two handsome young people of fortune. Slow motion on the deck of cards slipping out of Maria's hand and onto the floor.

The sound of Mrs. Norris's voice drifts into perceptual range as the young people examine each other.

MRS. NORRIS
And this is Julia (*Henry and Mary nod*) . . . who has just come
out into society this autumn, and Miss Maria Bertram, over
here . . . (*Henry smiles gallantly*) . . . has just became engaged
to Mr. Rushworth last month. Perhaps you passed Mr.
Rushworth's magnificent estate on your way in. The one
with the spectacular gardens. Sotherton?

RUSHWORTH

Actually, we're planning some improvements.

HENRY

Mr. Rushworth.

Mr. Rushworth remembers to close his mouth.

MRS. NORRIS
(without flourish)

And Fanny Price.

Henry struts in good-naturedly.

HENRY

Well, you certainly seem a dreary lot.

Everyone relaxes, except Mrs. Norris.

MRS. NORRIS

Oh no, Mr. Crawford, not in the least. These young people, if I could keep up with them, heavens . . . I'd be busier than the Prince of Wales.

Their collective amusement at Mrs. Norris's lack of humor binds them instantly.

MARIA

Please, do join us in our game. Mr. Crawford. . . .

*Rapid COLLAGE (slightly slowed down, focus in and out) of the young people
laughing, talking, eyeing and amusing each other.*

37 EXT. PATH TO PARSONAGE—AFTERNOON—A FEW HOURS LATER

Mary and Henry speak with quick, easy rapport.

MARY

Well?

HENRY

I like them both exceedingly.

MARY

Maria is in general the handsomest.

HENRY

She has the advantage in every feature. But I like Julia best.

MARY

Why?

HENRY

Because it must be so.

MARY

She certainly seems very ready to be fallen in love with.

HENRY

Though Maria is most agreeable.

MARY

Though her choice is made.

HENRY

Yes, and I like her the better for it. An engaged woman is
always more agreeable than a disengaged. She is satisfied
with herself. Her cares are over, and she feels that she may
exert all her powers of pleasing without suspicion. All is safe
with a lady engaged: No harm can be done.

MARY

You allow yourself great latitude on such points, Henry.
(taking his arm) But you will be the one taken in at last.

Mary glances back towards the Mansfield house to see Edmund looking out of the
east room window.

38   INT. FANNY'S ROOM—AFTERNOON

Fanny reads to Edmund, who is standing at the window. As she reads we see her
large collection of books and also her "works of ingenuity"—paper quilling, feather
and shell pictures, pinprick pictures, a picture of a ship made from sand.

FANNY

(urgent, amused)

'I cannot know if he loves me,' said Eliza. 'Well,' they asked,
'Did he never gaze on you with admiration—tenderly press
your hand—drop an involuntary tear—and leave the room
abruptly?' 'Never,' replied she. 'He has always left the room
indeed when his visit has been ended.' So, what do you
think?

EDMUND

(looking at Mary and Henry)

She's delightful. They are both delightful.

39   EXT. MANSFIELD—DAY—CONTINUOUS

Camera pans off Edmund at window over to another window in which we see Julia.

40   INT. MARIA'S BEDROOM/HALLWAY—
AFTERNOON—CONTINUOUS

Julia steps back from the window. Maria is lying on her bed languorously.

MARIA

There could be no harm in my liking an agreeable
man—everybody knows my situation—

JULIA

Must you always win, even when you already have your
prize?

Maria smiles and begins trying different hairstyles in the mirror.

MARIA

Julia, Julia, there will be little rubs and disappointments
everywhere. . . . If one scheme of happiness fails, human
nature turns to another.

Julia walks out the door down the hall to her own room.

JULIA

You may need your pretty philosophy in the end, Maria.

41 EXT. PATH TO PARSONAGE—
AFTERNOON—CONTINUOUS

> MARY

Pity Tom, the eldest, is not here.

> HENRY

What with his twenty thousand pounds and his baronetcy and all.

> MARY

Henry. (*smile*) You know those things mean nothing to me.

They walk away from camera.

> HENRY

Should we stay on awhile?

> MARY
> (*as in 'yes, please'*)

Mmm-hmmm.

42 INT. VARIOUS ROOMS OF MANSFIELD PARK—NEXT MORNING

Jump cut quick shots of everyone at Mansfield Park (Edmund, Maria, Julia, Lady Bertram) getting ready for the day, putting a little special attention into their appearance. Even Mrs. Norris shows up with a flower in her hair.

43 INT. STAIRCASE—MORNING—CONTINUOUS

Fanny notices something disturbing outside her window.

44 EXT. STABLES—MORNING—CONTINUOUS

Edmund has brought Mrs. Shakespeare outside and is showing Mary how to groom her. The atmosphere is somewhat charged.

45 EXT. MANSFIELD PARK GARDEN—MORNING—A HALF HOUR LATER

Mary is getting a lesson on Fanny's horse. Active and fearless and strongly made, she seems formed for a horsewoman. There is an extra attentiveness in Edmund's instruction of her.

45I INT. FANNY'S ROOM—MORNING

Fanny can hear the sound of their distant laughter. Fanny can't write.

46 EXT./INT. CONSERVATORY—MORNING—CONTINUOUS

Julia and Maria are playing a duet on an elaborate glass harmonica and for Henry in the glass-roofed conservatory. Mostly, Julia just provides the accompanying notes for Maria's flashy solos. Mrs. Norris, Rushworth and Lady Bertram look on approvingly. The music finishes sweetly.

> LADY BERTRAM
>
> I must say . . .

Camera ends on black sculpture of a slave.

> LADY BERTRAM (CONT'D)
>
> . . . the pleasures of life rarely transcend a moment such as this. Don't you agree, Pugsie?

SFX: a fragment of the sad sounds Fanny heard from the slave ship docked in Portsmouth Harbour.

Suddenly: LOUD HOOFBEATS.

47 DELETED

48 EXT. MANSFIELD—MORNING—CONTINUOUS

Tom and YATES, another dashing, reckless, rich boy, arrive on horseback. They kind of slide/fall off their horses. They haven't shaven and clearly have been drinking.

> MRS. NORRIS
>
> Tom, are you well, is there war? Where is Sir Thomas? What's the news? Edmund! Come quick!

> YATES
>
> Good morning, Mansfield.

Edmund arrives on horseback and dismounts quickly. Fanny looks out of her attic window.

                        EDMUND
What of Antigua? Where's father?

                        TOM
Ah, Antigua and all the lovely people there paying for this party. Yes.

                        JULIA
Tom, we thought you were in Antigua. Where are you coming from just now?

Tom burps.

                        MARIA
Please!

                        YATES
Tom returned from Antigua somewhat sooner than expected, so he spent a while in London. I found him in the green room of the Covent Garden Theatre.

                        EDMUND
In a theatre?

                        YATES
Yes. It happens to be where they are re-staging this delicious little slice of naughtiness called *Lover's Vows*.

                        HENRY
                      (positively)
Oh, I've heard of that.

                        YATES
Tom was a most charming parasite to the process until he

ran out of cash. And since I found myself quite capable of sympathizing with the tragedy of unwarranted poverty, I chose to deliver him to his family, whom I now discover to be so very loving and beautiful . . .

> TOM

> And solvent.

Mary arrives on Fanny's horse.

> MARY

> Ah, Mr. Bertram.

49   INT. BILLIARD ROOM—NEXT DAY

Fire burning. Tom, revived, is telling the story of Lover's Vows. *He has the book open in his hand. We read the title.*

The men and Mary are playing billiards. (NB: Lots of close-ups on the billiard balls being hit, missed or sunk throughout the conversation.) Julia and Maria are drinking tea.

Maria looks to see Lady Bertram yawning over her needlepoint with Fanny at her feet. Maria splashes a little sherry into her tea.

Julia casts admiring glances at Henry repeatedly. He refuses to notice.

> TOM

> So the baron makes love to the young country girl, Agatha. She is intoxicated with his fervent caresses, his whisperings and proddings, and finally succumbs to the delirium . . . until he plants into her willing—nay—wishing young body . . .

Tom is milking it. Henry smiles at Maria (was that a wink?). Julia catches it.

TOM

. . . an infant boy, Frederick. Then the baron leaves both lover and child. . . .

JULIA

And suffers the loss . . . ?

TOM

No, no, he has a most pleasant marriage, which produces a most attractive girl-child, Amelia, who becomes a not inconsequential lover herself, eventually seducing a clergyman, of all things. At any rate, the baron meets the bastard son, embraces him, takes back the lover of his youth, Agatha, and all live happily, it is presumed, for some time ever after.

YATES

Bravo, Tom.

HENRY

Well told, Mr. Bertram.

Edmund picks up the book and leafs through.

EDMUND

More dim-witted fiction to clutter the world.

MARY

Come now, Edmund. Drama is to life what . . . ships are to the sea, a means to traverse it, to plumb its depth, its breadth and its beauty.

EDMUND

I could not agree more, Mary. *Good* drama in which the greatest powers of the mind are displayed, in which the most thorough knowledge of human nature, the happiest delineation of its varieties, the liveliest effusion of wit and

humour are conveyed to the world in the best chosen
language, yes, this is essential. But this (*holding up* Lover's
Vows) . . . this is . . . trash.

Mary admires Edmund. He notices.

                              TOM

So serious.

                         EDMUND

That is the worst charge, isn't it, Tom?

*Henry sees Fanny nod in agreement with Edmund. Mrs. Norris enters. No one takes
much notice.*

                         HENRY

What do you think, Fanny Price?

                         FANNY

I'm sorry to disappoint, Mr. Crawford, but I do not have a
ready opinion.

                         HENRY

I suspect you are almost entirely composed of ready
opinions not shared.

Mrs. Norris notices this tender attention "wasted" on Fanny.

                    MRS. NORRIS

Fanny?

                         FANNY

Yes, Aunt Norris?

                    MRS. NORRIS

What are you doing here?

                         FANNY

Excuse me?

MRS. NORRIS

You are aware surely that the sewing wasn't cleared away from yesterday afternoon.

FANNY

(blushing)

You're quite right, Aunt Norris, it wasn't. I will see to it immediately.

EDMUND

(as in "shame on you")

Aunt Norris, surely the sewing can wait.

MRS. NORRIS

There's entirely . . . too much waiting in this household as it is.

Mortified, Fanny hurries out the door.

HENRY (OFFSCREEN)

Pray, is she out, or is she not?

The question seems never to have dawned on the Bertrams.

HENRY (CONT'D)

. . . into society . . .

MARIA (OFFSCREEN)

I can't see that it matters terribly.

50   INT. HALLWAY—DAY—CONTINUOUS

Fanny leans against the wall, angry and embarrassed.

51   INT. DRAWING ROOM—CONTINUOUS

YATES

Forget this out-not-out nonsense, I say we stage the play! Here, now, together.

TOM

Yates, you are a genius! This is the *very* room for a theatre,
and father's room will be an excellent greenroom.

RUSHWORTH

It has been mentioned that I have quite a gift for the stage,
actually.

EDMUND

You are not serious, Tom.

TOM

Not serious! Me?!

EDMUND

Lover's Vows? I am convinced that our father would
disapprove, Tom.

TOM
(displeased)
I know my father as well as you do. Manage your own
concerns, Edmund, and I'll take care of the rest of the family.
Don't act yourself, if you do not like it, but don't expect to
govern everybody else. That's settled then. Good.

*Tom slams his hand on Lady Bertram's chair back. She, the picture of health, wealth,
ease, and tranquillity, wakes with a start. Edmund smiles and shakes his head.*

LADY BERTRAM
(waking)
What! What is the matter? *(everyone laughs)* I was not
asleep!

TOM

Oh dear, no, ma'am, nobody suspected you!

LADY BERTRAM

I must have dropped off. Where's Fanny? Mrs. Norris, get me Fanny Price.

Mrs. Norris scowls. Edmund stirs the fire in agitated vexation.

MARY

I wish to play Amelia, but what I am keen to know is what gentleman (*looking from Tom to Edmund*) among you am I to have the pleasure of making love to?

General startledness around the room.

52 INT. FANNY'S ROOM—DAY—LATER

Edmund is pacing back and forth.

EDMUND

How has it happened that the wish to do what is right became an unattractive quality? Now Tom wants to enlist Charles Maddox to play Anhalt. He is about as discreet as the town crier. . . .

There is a knock at the door. It is Mary, looking ravishing as ever.

MARY

So this is where you hide. Fanny, I need some rehearsing, could you . . . Oh, Mr. Bertram, hello.

EDMUND

Hello, Miss Crawford. I'll be off then, Fanny.

MARY

Stay. Stay. We need an audience. We all need an audience, wouldn't you say, Fanny?

FANNY

To be truthful, I live in dread of audiences.

Fanny's hesitation is taken as acquiescence.

MARY

Come, here. (*handing her the play*) I will play Amelia and you, for now, will play Anhalt the clergyman, my teacher. Read from here. Since Mr. Bertram here refuses.

FANNY

No, please . . .

MARY

I insist.

FANNY

I'm not . . .

She looks to Edmund, who seems to think it is all right.

Fanny takes the play from her. Edmund sits in Fanny's reading chair.

MARY/AMELIA

"For a long time you have instructed me, why should not I
begin to teach you?"

FANNY/ANHALT

"Teach me what?"

MARY/AMELIA

"Whatever I know, and you don't."

FANNY/ANHALT

"There are some things I had rather never know."

MARY/AMELIA

"Just as you make certain mathematical problems pleasant
to me, I might teach something as pleasant to you."

*Mary is standing extremely close to Fanny, touching her occasionally. Edmund
watches attentively.*

FANNY/ANHALT

"Woman herself is a problem."

MARY/AMELIA

"And I'll teach you to make her out."

FANNY/ANHALT

"*You* teach?"

MARY/AMELIA

"Why not? None but a woman can teach the science of
herself."

*Mary puts her arms around Fanny's neck. Fanny stands there, stiff as a board,
blushing entirely at Mary's tenderness.*

Edmund stands up.

EDMUND

Upon reconsideration, I cannot help but think, despite the displeasure of appearing inconsistent, it would be better for me to play Anhalt than to invite Maddox into this mixture.

Mary's smile broadens.

MARY

Excellent.

CU on Fanny most surprised, and a bit betrayed.

53 INT. BILLIARD ROOM—A FEW DAYS LATER—NIGHT

Fanny wanders into the billiard room and communicating rooms (i.e., study/hall/ "backstage area") watching the intense industry of the upcoming theatrical adventure.

Yates is directing the carpenters to put the finishing touches on two wings to the stage. Sawdust is everywhere.

Mrs. Norris is admiring the baize curtain fabric.

MRS. NORRIS

Hmmm, this is less than I ordered. . . .

Backstage, Fanny comes upon Henry and Maria (heavily made up) "acting" outrageously. Neither of them can completely contain a smile in all of this.

HENRY/FREDERICK

Mother!

MARIA/AGATHA

Frederick!

HENRY/FREDERICK

Mother! For God's sake what is this! How is this! And why
do I find my mother thus! Speak!

He holds her tightly.

*Through a gap we see Julia, dampening the gauze on her bosom with water to
make it a little more transparent. She rounds the corner to see Maria and Henry.*

MARIA/AGATHA
(kissing his face)
I cannot speak, dear son! My dear Frederick! The joy is too
great—I was not prepared—

HENRY/FREDERICK

Dear mother, compose yourself. (*leans his head against her
breast*) Now, then, be comforted. How she trembles! She is
fainting.

*Fanny quickly moves on, afraid of being embarrassed by their "acting." Julia walks
off in a huff.*

Mary and Edmund stand close together, practicing lines.

*In a corner, Fanny sees Sir Thomas's papers. She picks up the lithograph of the slave
and brushes off the sawdust.*

*SFX: Outside we hear horses. The sound of hammering covers the noise. Fanny
thinks she hears something.*

54 INT. HALLWAY—NIGHT

*Fanny, seeking out the source of the sound she heard, comes across Julia, sobbing.
Fanny stands behind her with her hand hovering over Julia's shoulder, not certain
whether to comfort her. She finally does.*

FANNY

Julia . . .

Julia shrugs Fanny's hand off her shoulder brusquely.

JULIA

Don't *you* pity me too.

She leaves. Fanny aches for the both of them.

55 EXT. MANSFIELD PARK—NIGHT—CONTINUOUS

Sir Thomas's post-chaise arrives in the darkness.

56 INT. BILLIARD ROOM/SIR THOMAS'S STUDY—NIGHT—CONTINUOUS

Tom, made up in crude black-face, is finishing applying rouge to Yates's face.

TOM

Now, where is Edmund, Mr. Moral Pillar himself?

57 EXT. MANSFIELD PARK—NIGHT—CONTINUOUS

Sir Thomas climbs out of the carriage.

58 INT. ENTRANCE HALL—NIGHT—CONTINUOUS

Sir Thomas enters. He has the burnt, worn look of fatigue and a hot climate. Fanny comes into the hall. She stops and stares.

FANNY

Welcome home, sir.

He takes her in his arms and gives her a hug, as if trying to absorb some of her innocence. She is surprised by his warmth.

SIR THOMAS

Hello my sweet, dear girl. . . . my word, you have grown in health and, I dare say, beauty. Where is my gentle family? *(hears banging sounds)* What is that?

FANNY

Umm, it's . . . sir . . .

SIR THOMAS

Improvements?

He doesn't wait for her answer and heads towards the source of the noise.

59 INT. BILLIARD ROOM/SIR THOMAS'S STUDY—NIGHT—CONTINUOUS

Sir Thomas enters via the backstage area to see his books in a heap in a corner and the billiard table upended, with a tear in the green. The papers from his desk are in a pile underneath.

Julia, now in the wings, is shooting back a drink. Henry and Maria are pressed up against each other, almost kissing. Rushworth is adjusting his hose admiringly in a mirror.

RUSHWORTH

Oh, you must be Sir Thomas, yes, I am Rushworth, your future son-in-law. *(shakes his hand vigorously)* We are in the

midst of a home theatrical. I am to be Count Cassel, and
am to come in first with a blue dress and a pink satin cloak,
and afterwards am to have another fine fancy suit, by way
of a shooting-dress. I have two and forty speeches, which is
no trifle.

*One by one everyone in the room notices Sir Thomas's presence. Silence sweeps
into the room, like a rush of wind blowing out all the candles of a chandelier.*

Sir Thomas says nothing. His disapproval is evident.

*Henry and Mary glance at each other. All begin wiping the makeup off their faces,
leaving ghoulish streaks. Yates enters stage left and delivers his most convincing
"startled stare" yet.*

Sir Thomas looks to Edmund.

                            EDMUND
     Sir, it's just a play. . . .

Sir Thomas raises his hand to silence him. He lowers his head.

Mrs. Norris, when she sees through his eyes, feels the error in her own judgment.

Mary and Henry quietly depart behind the wings of the stage.

*Tom, in smeared blackface, enters the room and finds himself face to face with Sir
Thomas.*

                         SIR THOMAS
     Ah, Tom. So this is what you were in such a terrible hurry
     to leave Antigua for, I presume.

*Tom turns to leave. He flips over a small table of food on his way out. This wakes
up Lady Bertram.*

LADY BERTRAM

Oh, Sir Thomas, I could not have borne your absence a moment longer!

60 EXT. INNER COURT AND STABLES—NEXT DAY—DAWN

Tom and Yates sneak off in one of Sir Thomas's carriages in the early morning.

FANNY (VOICE-OVER)

Dear Susy: All remnants of the theatre have been erased.

61 INT. DRAWING ROOM—THAT NIGHT

Henry, Mary, Maria, Rushworth, Edmund, Fanny, Mrs. Norris and Lady Bertram are listening to Sir Thomas's tales of Antigua. The time passes heavily.

FANNY (VOICE-OVER)

And a certain solemnity has returned to Mansfield Park. . . .

Maria is touching Henry's foot with hers under the table. He seems bored. Rushworth can't resist adjusting his hair in the mirror. Fanny, who is serving tarts, is very interested in the discussion.

SIR THOMAS

The mulattos are in general well-shaped and the women especially well-featured. I have one—so easy and graceful in her movements and intelligent as well. . . . But strangely, you know, two mulattos will never have children. They are of the mule-kind in that respect.

Fanny and Edmund exchange a look.

EDMUND

Excuse me, Father, for contradicting you, but that is
nonsense—you cannot say such things.

SIR THOMAS

I did not say they *are* mules, did I? I said they were *like*
mules. Edward Long's *History of Jamaica*—read it before you
challenge me, son. Anyway, I have a good mind to bring back
one of them next trip to work here as a domestic.

FANNY

(as she serves him some tart)

Correct me if I am in error, Sir Thomas, but I've read, sir,
that if you were to bring one of the slaves back to England,
there would be some argument as to whether or not they
should be freed here . . .

A dead silence. Everyone turns to look at Fanny, who so rarely initiates any subject
in public, let alone one of such significance.

FANNY

. . . if I'm not mistaken.

SIR THOMAS

I must say you have changed considerably, my dear.

FANNY

I have done some reading on the matter. Thomas Clarkson
to be specific. Under Edmund's guidance.

EDMUND

Fanny has a voracious mind. As hungry as any man's, father.

Henry notices her adoration of Edmund.

FANNY

'Twas you who charmed my intelligence, Edmund.

EDMUND

Her writing is remarkable, in a style entirely new.

SIR THOMAS

(as if he'd heard nothing)

Yes, good . . . yes, your complexion is so improved.

EDMUND

(offended on her behalf)

I trust you will see as much beauty of mind in time, father.

He hears nothing and just looks her over. It makes Fanny extremely uncomfortable.

SIR THOMAS

. . . You have gained so much countenance, and your
figure . . .

FANNY

Please . . .

SIR THOMAS

Don't you agree, Mr. Crawford?

HENRY

Purity is a decided attraction, it is true, Sir Thomas.

MARIA

(under her breath)

Especially for the impure.

Maria looks away.

SIR THOMAS

Indeed.

HENRY

It must be the moral taste and the steadfastness of her heart
that illuminate her eyes and give such a glow to her cheek.

FANNY

Please.

MARY

Gentlemen, Fanny Price is almost as fearful of notice and
praise as other women are of neglect.

EDMUND

Most discerning, Miss Crawford.

MARY

Thank you, Mr. Bertram.

They glow at each other for a moment. Fanny, still squirming under all the attention,
sees this and feels worse.

SIR THOMAS

I have it! I know that under my government, Mansfield is an
altered place and my return has dampened your youthful
energies, but I have the solution. A ball at Mansfield Park! In
honor of Fanny. We shall bring her out and introduce Miss
Fanny Price to society.

Everyone, excluding Fanny and Maria, bursts into applause and cheers.

SIR THOMAS (CONT'D)

Surely some young man of good standing will sit up and take
notice.

HENRY

I am certain she will glide about with quiet, light elegance
and in admirable time.

Fanny gets up to leave.

FANNY

You must excuse me. I think I have something . . . Excuse
me.

Edmund, sensing her unease, follows.

SIR THOMAS

It needn't be a large affair, just a few neighbors and friends.

He glances at Henry.

62 EXT. MANSFIELD PARK—NIGHT—CONTINUOUS

Fanny runs through the rain to the stables. Edmund follows close behind.

63 INT. STABLES—NIGHT—CONTINUOUS

Fanny is tacking up Mrs. Shakespeare for a ride.

EDMUND

Don't be foolish, Fanny, it is raining.

FANNY

I see more distinctly through rain.

EDMUND

It's just a silly ball.

FANNY

I'll not be sold off like one of your father's slaves, Edmund.

EDMUND

Don't be an imbecile!

FANNY

Oh, but imbecility in females is a great enhancement to their personal charms.

EDMUND

You are being irrational.

FANNY

Yet another adornment. I must be ravishing.

Fanny mounts the horse. She has used Edmund's saddle.

EDMUND

Fanny! You must really begin to harden yourself to the idea of . . .

She rides off astride her horse.

EDMUND (CONT'D)

. . . being worth looking at.

64   EXT. FIELD—NIGHT—CONTINUOUS

Fanny, crying, charges through the rain.

65   EXT. MANSFIELD PARK—NIGHT—A FEW MOMENTS LATER

Edmund returns to the gathering. Through the window he sees his father speaking with Mary. Sir Thomas is laughing in delight.

66 EXT. COTTAGE NEAR MANSFIELD PARK— THAT NIGHT

Fanny comes out of the wood and upon a very small farmer's cottage lit by its hearth. She can see, just barely through a curtain, a man and woman reclining on a carpet in front of the fire. They've just eaten. The infant between them is nursing. It is a small stolen view of what seems like perfect domestic joy.

Something in this joy saddens our heroine even more.

67 INT. DRAWING ROOM—SAME NIGHT

Sir Thomas comes up behind Edmund, who is standing alone looking out the window.

> SIR THOMAS
>
> You could do worse, Edmund.

> EDMUND
>
> Sir?

> SIR THOMAS
>
> She is witty and bright and I dare say not without . . . worth.

> EDMUND
>
> And how might you measure that worth, Father?

> SIR THOMAS
>
> Oh, you need not impress me with your purity, son. Her family is well established. It is well known.

> EDMUND
> *(baffled)*
>
> The Prices?

Sir Thomas looks at him with some surprise.

                              SIR THOMAS
      The Crawfords, Edmund. I meant the Crawfords. Mary
      Crawford.

They exchange a long and solemn look.

68   INT. LIBRARY—THAT NIGHT

Fanny stands near the window. Her hair is still a little wet from her night ride. She is reading. Henry knocks.

                              FANNY
      Yes?

                              HENRY
      May I enter?

                              FANNY
      Yes.

                              HENRY
      What are you reading?

                              FANNY
      Laurence Sterne's A *Sentimental Journey.*

                              HENRY
      May I?

                              FANNY
      As you wish.

                              HENRY
                          (reads aloud)
      "I was interrupted . . . with a voice which I took to be of a

child, which complained it could not get out. I looked up and down the passage and saw it was a starling hung in a little cage.—'I can't get out—I can't get out,' said the starling."

His reading is fluid and surprisingly sincere.

> HENRY (CONT'D)
> " 'God help thee!' said I, 'but I'll let thee out, cost what it will.' But it was double-twisted with wire and there was no getting it open without pulling the cage to pieces—I took both hands to it."

Through the crack in the door we see Maria, also listening.

> HENRY (CONT'D)
> "The bird flew to the place where I was attempting his deliverance, and thrusting his head through the trellis, pressed his breast against it, as if impatient—I fear, poor creature! said I, I cannot set thee at liberty—"

Henry looks into Fanny's eyes.

> HENRY (CONT'D)
> " 'No,' said the starling, 'I can't get out—I can't get out,' said the starling."

Fanny is moved, as is Henry. Finally, she looks away.

> FANNY
> You read well.

> HENRY
> Thank you.

Maria too is affected by the sentiment. She turns away and retreats into the darkness.

69 EXT. MANSFIELD PARK—NIGHT

We see Maria's silhouette. She is pacing alone in her room.

70 INT. SIR THOMAS'S STUDY—NEXT MORNING

Maria stands before Sir Thomas.

MARIA

Father, I wish to speak to you about Rushworth.

SIR THOMAS

Ah, Maria, you know how eagerly disposed I was to like
your Mr. Rushworth. . . .

MARIA

But you think him an inferior young man, as ignorant in
business as in books, with opinions in general unfixed, and
without seeming much aware of it himself.

SIR THOMAS

Uh . . . well (*he nods*).

MARIA

I am not blind, Father.

SIR THOMAS

Perhaps the alliance, as advantageous as it is, was too
quickly agreed to. You need not worry, Maria, I shall take
care of you, every inconvenience should be braved, and the
connection entirely given up, if you feel yourself unhappy in
the prospect of it.

MARIA

I will not pretend he is of shining character. But I will also not pretend that enjoying a larger income and a house in the city and all the other amiable and innocent enjoyments the connection will afford are not an attraction. For the rest, well, he is still young. And (*beat*) I wish to marry him immediately. Within a fortnight.

> SIR THOMAS

I don't understand the urgency.

> MARIA

I don't understand the delay. And I wish for Julia to accompany me on the honeymoon.

> SIR THOMAS

And you wish for Julia to accompany you on your honeymoon?

> MARIA

Yes, she has never been to Brighton.

71   EXT. PARSONAGE—DUSK

Men are working madly to get in the hay. A large, ornate harp strapped to the top of Henry's barouche enters the frame.

72   INT. CHURCH—TWO WEEKS LATER—DAY

Maria is approaching the altar looking beautiful. Rushworth waits for her there. DR. GRANT reads the service.

73 INT. FANNY'S ROOM—NIGHT

> FANNY (TO CAMERA)
>
> Dear Susy: Maria was married on Saturday. In all the important preparations of mind she was complete: being prepared for matrimony by a hatred of home, by the misery of disappointed affection and contempt of the man she was to marry.

74 INT. CHURCH—DAY

We see Rushworth and Maria at the altar with bridesmaids. They turn toward the church. Rushworth smiles at Maria gormlessly. She can barely resist rolling her eyes.

> FANNY (VOICE-OVER)
>
> The bride was elegantly dressed and the two bridesmaids were duly inferior.

Cut to: Lady Bertram looking tired.

> FANNY (VOICE-OVER)
>
> Her mother stood with salts in her hand, expecting to be agitated . . .

Cut to: Mrs. Norris.

> FANNY (VOICE-OVER, CONT'D)
>
> . . . and her aunt tried to cry.

75 EXT. SOTHERTON—DAY—A FEW HOURS LATER

We watch the carriage with Maria, Rushworth and Julia drive off. Maria sneaks one last look out at Henry. Lady Bertram gives Fanny a squeeze.

It is a comfort to think *you* will never leave us, Fanny.

76 EXT. PARSONAGE—DAY—A FEW WEEKS LATER

Hard rain. Fanny, carrying a basket of blackberries, tries to take shelter under an oak tree.

77 EXT. PARSONAGE PARLOUR—DAY—CONTINUOUS

Mary, looking out the window, notices Fanny outside. (NB: camera outside looking in.)

78 EXT. PARSONAGE—DAY—CONTINUOUS

Mary rushes out with an umbrella and escorts her in.

79 INT. PARSONAGE VESTIBULE—DAY—MOMENTS LATER

Mary admires Fanny, dripping wet.

MARY

Ah, Fanny!

FANNY

I should bring these blackberries to Mrs. Norris.

MARY

No, I shall be selfish and keep you here to stay and play
with me. She must forgive me. Selfishness must always be
forgiven, you know, because there is no hope of a cure.

80 INT. PARSONAGE/MARY'S ROOM—MOMENTS LATER

Mary undresses Fanny, who is shy but overwhelmed by Mary's industrious delight in helping.

MARY

Oh, yes, this is lovely. Tomorrow evening, the ballroom shall
be lit solely by your beauty.

FANNY

Please, Miss Crawford . . .

MARY

You do have a fine form, my dear. I have no wonder that
Edmund delights so in your company.

Mary dresses Fanny in her own clothes.

MARY (CONT'D)

I'm so evil he knows not what to make of me. Would that I
had your sound judgment. Tell me . . . does he speak of
me . . . ?

                              FANNY

Occasionally. (*changing the subject*) Is that your harp in the
drawing room?

                              MARY

Indeed, it was transported from London on Henry's
barouche. I tried to hire a horse and cart but I found that I
had been asking the most unreasonable, most impossible
thing in the world. I had offended all the farmers, all the
laborers, all the hay in the parish!

                              FANNY

Getting the hay in is of great importance in the country at
this time.

                              MARY

And music isn't?

                              FANNY

Depends on the music, I suppose.

81   INT. PARSONAGE/PARLOUR—MOMENTS LATER

Mary plays beautifully.

                              MARY

This is Edmund's favorite. He seems very alive to music.

Edmund appears at the door. They are both unaware.

                              FANNY

Yes, Edmund says that in a church service, it is music that
best allows the spirit to aspire to the beyond.

                              MARY

Heavens, why waste it on drowsy church-goers starched up

into seeming piety. Give me a concert or a dance. I'm sure he would agree.

FANNY

Forgive my contradiction, Miss Crawford, but I'm sure he wouldn't. When (*pointedly*) he takes orders in a few weeks he will begin, if I'm not mistaken, his own services.

MARY

Take orders! What, is Edmund to be a clergyman?

FANNY

Yes.

MARY

But a clergyman is nothing! And a clergyman's wife is barely half that!

Edmund steps into the room.

EDMUND

What profession would you suggest, Miss Crawford? I am not, as you know, the firstborn.

MARY

There must be some uncle or grandfather to get you in somewhere.

EDMUND

There is not.

MARY

Choose law then, it is not too late. At least you can distinguish yourself there with language and wit.

EDMUND

I have no wish to blunder about on the borders of empty repartee.

MARY (CONT'D)

Or your father could put you into Parliament.

EDMUND

My father's choices are less than compelling for me.

Edmund stands up, walks close to her. He plucks the strings of the harp lightly once or twice as he speaks.

EDMUND

No, I wish to be a clergyman. Even if I find some of the speculations of the trade somewhat fanciful, I think there are many things worse than a life of compassion and contemplation.

Mary and Edmund lock eyes.

MARY

(a bit shaken)

You must excuse me. I have been frightfully rude to Mrs. Eaton, she invited me to her house on the coast a full fortnight ago, and I have yet to respond.

Edmund and Fanny can barely believe the transparency of her dismissal.

EDMUND

Miss Crawford . . .

MARY

Excuse me, please.

Edmund and Fanny get up to go.

82   EXT. PATH BETWEEN MANSFIELD HOUSE AND PARSONAGE—DAY

Fanny and Edmund walk home in the light rain.

> EDMUND
>
> She does not think evil, but she speaks it. And it grieves me to the soul.

> FANNY
>
> The effect of education, perhaps.

He takes her arm.

> EDMUND
>
> Perhaps she can be de-educated. (*Fanny smiles*) Oh, Fanny, would that more women were like you. I love you beyond the power of words to express. I demand the first dance at the ball tomorrow.

Fanny leans into him just little.

83   INT. FANNY'S ROOM—NEXT NIGHT—AFTERNOON

Fanny lies in bed. From the ever-so-subtle movements of her covers we suspect she may be touching herself.

84   INT. GREAT HALL—THAT NIGHT

Fanny, dressed all in white, twirls wildly in Edmund's arms. They play as if they were children again. Her cheeks are flushed. A drop of wax from the candles in the chandelier above just misses her.

Sir Thomas and Henry and a few others admire her. Fanny sees that she is approved; and the consciousness of looking well makes her look still better.

Another young man steps towards them as if to step in for the next piece. Fanny steers Edmund away to avoid him.

FANNY

(to Edmund)

One's consequence varies so much at times without any particular reason.

EDMUND

There is reason for everything, Fanny: Your entire person is entirely agreeable.

FANNY

And tonight I agree with everyone.

Edmund swings her again. They laugh out loud.

Henry steps up for the next dance. Edmund steps back. Before they start, Fanny reaches over to a table and takes a sip from her drink. The quartet launches into a faster piece.

Edmund approaches Mary. Fanny overhears.

EDMUND

Will you dance with me?

MARY

Yes. (*Edmund smiles in relief*) But it is the last time I will ever dance with you. I have never danced with a clergyman and never will.

It is all said through smiles, so Edmund does not know how to receive her comments. They dance.

Henry and Fanny make a lovely couple on the dance floor. Effortless grace.

HENRY

You dance like an angel, Fanny Price.

FANNY

One does not dance like an angel alone.

HENRY

What?! A compliment! Let the heavens rejoice! She complimented me.

FANNY

I complimented your dancing, Mr. Crawford. Keep your wig on.

He laughs. She laughs. The tempo speeds up and they are off again.

Sir Thomas and Mrs. Norris look at Henry and Fanny and smile approvingly. Mary shares a look with Henry. They smile.

Mary leans in to whisper something in Edmund's ear.

> MARY
>
> I think you should admit you are in love with Fanny Price, Edmund.

> EDMUND
>
> Of course I love her, Mary. (*another turn*) But there are as many forms of love as there are moments in time.

The musicians, seemingly caught up in the intoxication of the evening, look at each other and the music speeds up again. Other couples drop out.

Edmund steals a glance at Fanny. Is that a look of jealousy? Fanny glances at Edmund, then Mary. Henry glances at the wild pulse in Fanny's neck. Fanny surveys Edmund's dashing form. Henry's hand slips down Fanny's back just slightly.

The symphony of glances speeds up until we don't know who is looking at whom.

Finally, Fanny, in slow motion, closes her eyes.

SFX: sound of her breathing heavily.

Cut quickly between disorientingly rapid shots of Fanny dancing with Edmund, then Henry, then Edmund, then Sir Thomas, then another, then Edmund, then Henry.

The wax from another chandelier drips again. Slowly down, down and down. But tonight no one is hurt.

A few people leave, the party begins to dwindle. Fanny runs up the stairs laughing. Both Edmund and Henry notice her departure, from different points in the room.

85   INT. STAIRWELL—NIGHT

Fanny shakes her head and opens her eyes as she weaves her way up to bed after the dance, feverish with hopes and fears, soup and drink.

86   INT. FANNY'S ROOM—NIGHT

Fanny stumbles into her room. She picks up some of her papers from her desk and smiles to herself. She reads back her story out loud:

> FANNY
>
> "And then, a few hours before Laura died, she said, 'Take warning from my unhappy end. . . . Beware of fainting fits and beware of swoons. . . .' "

She looks out at the full moon. Carriages are pulling away. People are laughing.

87   INT. FANNY'S ROOM/FRONT OF MANSFIELD PARK—NIGHT—CONTINUOUS

Fanny looks outside and sees someone step out of the shadows and look up at her. It is Henry. They exchange a long, grave look.

88   EXT. MANSFIELD PARK—NIGHT—CONTINUOUS

Finally she snuffs the candles on her desk, which makes her invisible to him. They both continue to look at each other. In the dark she recites the rest of her story:

> FANNY
>
> *(whispered)*
>
> "Run mad as often as you choose, but do not faint—"

The four young people (Fanny, Henry, Mary and Edmund) sit around a card table. Fanny seems more confident. (NB: Lots of close-ups on the cards during this scene.)

Sir Thomas comes in and sets himself down with a liqueur beside the snoozing Lady Bertram and her pug.

> FANNY, HENRY, MARY, EDMUND
> Father, Good evening, hello, welcome (etc.)

> HENRY
> *(dealing)*
> Sir Thomas, I've been thinking about the parsonage.

> MARY
> Not you too.

Edmund smiles ruefully at Mary. He turns over a two of spades.

> HENRY
> Ah, spades is trump. Fanny . . . *(indicating she should take her turn)* I'm all in the glow, Sir Thomas, of a new scheme.

> SIR THOMAS
> What might that be?

> HENRY
> *(to Sir Thomas)*
> I thought you might be amenable to renting the parsonage to me.

Fanny looks up from her cards.

> FANNY
> But it is to be Edmund's parsonage when he takes his orders.

MARY

Anyone care to purchase a queen?

EDMUND

At what cost?

MARY

Ten pence.

EDMUND

Highway robbery.

HENRY

Mr. Bertram (*indicating Edmund*) could continue here at Mansfield Park and still be preacher. (*turning a card*) Hmm. The knave still hasn't presented himself. (*to Edmund*) This way you stay closer to your dear family. And I continue, improving and *perfecting* that friendship and (*Henry glances at Fanny*) intimacy with the Mansfield Park family, which is increasing in value to me every day.

Sir Thomas gets up and puts his hand on Henry's shoulder.

SIR THOMAS

I have a better plan, Henry. Live here, with us, stay as long as you wish every season. Bring all your horses. And your sister too. Be as one of our family. We would thrive on it, wouldn't we, Fanny?

FANNY

Of course. Who'll buy the ace for twenty-five?

MARY

I will.

HENRY

Mary, it's exorbitant!

MARY

I will stake my last like a woman of spirit. No cold prudence
for me. I am not born to sit still and do nothing. If I lose the
game, it shall not be from not striving for it.

*The transaction is executed. But then Fanny puts down the knave. General "oohs"
and "ahs." She collects the pot.*

90 INT. DRAWING ROOM—DAY—MOMENTS LATER

Fanny has just left the room and is on her way upstairs. Henry comes out after her.

HENRY

Fanny! Fanny! I must speak to you.

FANNY

Yes, Mr. Crawford.

HENRY

You must know why I am attempting to rent the
parsonage—I wish to "continue, improve and perfect my
intimacy" . . . with you.

Fanny is at first surprised and flattered by his candor, then dismisses it.

HENRY (CONT'D)

Fanny, you have created sensations which my heart had
never known before.

FANNY

Please . . .

HENRY

There is only one happiness in life, to love and be loved.

FANNY

(on the way upstairs)

Mr. Crawford, do not speak nonsense.

HENRY

Nonsense?!

FANNY

You are such a fine speaker that I'm afraid you may end in
actually convincing yourself.

HENRY

Fanny, you are killing me. . . .

FANNY

No man dies of love but on the stage, Mr. Crawford.

She leaves, shaking her head at what must be merely some aggressive flirting.

91   INT. FANNY'S ROOM—THAT NIGHT

Fanny sits in her nightgown. She is writing; having fun.

FANNY (CONT'D)

"From this period, the intimacy between them daily
increased till at length it grew to such a pitch, that they did
not scruple to kick one another out of the window on the
slightest provocation."

SFX: She hears the heavy thud of steps coming toward her room. There's a knock
at her door.

She pulls on a dressing gown to cover herself. He knocks.

FANNY

Yes?

Sir Thomas enters.

SIR THOMAS

Ahh, my sweet girl.

He looks at her as if examining a lovely jewel.

SIR THOMAS (CONT'D)

This is a great day. A great day indeed.

FANNY

It is?

SIR THOMAS

You may make me more proud, I dare say, than my own
daughters.

FANNY

Oh, please don't say that, sir.

SIR THOMAS
(suddenly chilled)

Why have you no fire today?

FANNY

I am not cold, sir.

SIR THOMAS

But you have a fire in general.

FANNY

No sir. But I have a warm shawl.

SIR THOMAS

Your aunt cannot be aware of this.

Fanny doesn't know what to say.

SIR THOMAS (CONT'D)

I understand. For as long as you are in my home, Fanny
Price, you shall have a fire.

He takes a deep breath.

SIR THOMAS (CONT'D)
(important manner)

I am aware that there has been a misplaced distinction but
I think too well of you, Fanny Price, to suppose you will
ever harbor resentment on that account. Thus it is with all
the more pleasure, then, that I am here to inform you that
Henry Crawford has asked my permission to take your
hand in marriage, Miss Fanny Price. And I have given the
union my blessing.

Fanny reels. She sits down.

Fanny can only shake her head a little.

SIR THOMAS (CONT'D)

I had no idea that his feelings had progressed to such a
boiling point. Clearly, I am too old to follow the intricate
maneuverings of the young.

Fanny is still in shock. He opens the door grandly.

SIR THOMAS (CONT'D)

Please accompany me downstairs. Mr. Crawford, as you
have perhaps foreseen, is yet in the house.

She doesn't come to him so he goes to her and kisses her tenderly on the forehead.

SIR THOMAS (CONT'D)

Do not fear.

FANNY

I cannot, sir.

SIR THOMAS

Cannot what?

FANNY

I cannot . . . agree to marry him . . . at this time.

SIR THOMAS

You do not know your own feelings. I've watched you with him, Fanny Price, I know you are not insensitive to his charms. I am not *that* old.

FANNY

He is not without charm, sir.

SIR THOMAS

Has someone else declared his intentions for you?

FANNY

No sir.

SIR THOMAS
(impatient)

Then what is it?

FANNY

I do not . . . trust him, sir.

SIR THOMAS

What do you distrust?

FANNY

His nature, sir. Like many charming people he conceals an
almost absolute dependence on the appreciation of others.

SIR THOMAS

And what can be the terrible ill of that?

FANNY

His sole interest is in being loved, sir, not in loving.

SIR THOMAS

You have read too many novels, girl.

FANNY

I am an unabashed novel reader, sir, but I do not think it has
clouded my judgment.

He paces about madly.

SIR THOMAS

Do you trust me?

FANNY

I trust that my future is entirely dependent upon you, sir.

SIR THOMAS

Let me repeat: Do you trust me?

FANNY

Yes, sir.

SIR THOMAS

Well, *I* trust *him*. (*leaning in to her*) You will marry him.

FANNY

I will not. (*beat*) Sir.

They stare at each other.

92 EXT. FIELD—SAME NIGHT

Henry and Mary ride under the large harvest moon, Mary on Fanny's horse.

> HENRY
>
> I am determined to marry Fanny Price.

> MARY
>
> Henry!

> HENRY
>
> The pleasing plague has finally stolen me, Mary. Her gentle manners, her high notion of honor, her unbearably sweet temper . . . that soft skin of hers. But there is something more. I so want her to . . . look kindly on me.

> MARY
>
> Perhaps, foolish boy, it is her *not* caring about you which gives her such soft skin and all these charms and graces.

> HENRY
>
> Whatever the reason, the effect is the same: I love her.

> MARY
>
> Is this the same Henry Crawford?

> HENRY
>
> No, it is a new Henry Crawford.

93 INT. SIR THOMAS'S STUDY—NEXT DAY

Fanny now sits in Sir Thomas's study. Sir Thomas is controlling his anger.

> SIR THOMAS
>
> I *had,* Fanny Price, thought you peculiarly free from

willfulness of temper, self-conceit and every tendency to that independence of spirit which prevails so much in modern days, even in young women, and which in young women is especially offensive and disgusting beyond all common offense.

Fanny, wounded by his criticism, looks as if she may cry.

94   INT. CONSERVATORY—DAY

Sir Thomas's harangue continues. (The impression must be of an uninterrupted monologue that continues through the following day.) Fanny, head bowed, is sitting in front of her uneaten lunch. Lady Bertram and Edmund are listening.

> SIR THOMAS (CONT'D)
> You seem to have forgotten that you do not have Mary Crawford's annual income, for example. Nor does your family. Their advantage or disadvantage never seems to have had a moment's share in your thoughts on this occasion.

Fanny looks at Edmund, he looks away.

Mrs. Norris is saying as much as possible without saying anything.

Fanny looks out of the window at Mary and Edmund walking and talking in intimate confidence. They laugh.

> SIR THOMAS (CONT'D)
> You think only of yourself, and because you do not feel for
> Mr. Crawford exactly what a young heated fancy imagines
> to be necessary for happiness . . .

> MRS. NORRIS
> I'd say not . . .

Sir Thomas raises his hand to silence Mrs. Norris.

Outside, Henry joins Mary and Edmund. He is looking forlorn. They comfort him. He glances at the window and sees Fanny. They exchange a sad expression. She turns away.

> SIR THOMAS
> . . . and are, in a wild fit of folly, throwing away from you
> such an opportunity of being settled in life, eligibly,
> honorably, nobly settled, as will, probably, never occur to
> you again.

LATER:

Reveal that Mary and Edmund now sit inside with Sir Thomas and Fanny, their cheeks rosy from the walk and from their pleasure in each other.

> LADY BERTRAM
> And I will tell you what, Fanny Price—which is more than I
> did for Maria—the next time the pug has a litter you shall
> have a puppy.

They all look patient.

MARY

All she needs is time, Sir Thomas. He loves you, Fanny Price, if any man ever loved a woman forever, I think Henry will do as much for you.

Fanny looks pleadingly at Edmund, seeking his support.

FANNY

Edmund? What are your thoughts?

EDMUND

Fanny, (*taking her hand*) the fact that he chose *you* is evidence of his good character. He could make you very happy, and you would be the making of him.

She stares at him, tears welling up, betrayed.

FANNY

I think it ought not to be set down as certain, that a man must be acceptable to every woman he may happen to like himself.

Sir Thomas rises up in anger.

SIR THOMAS

Perhaps you would rather return to Portsmouth? I can write to your mother tonight. (*long pause*) A little abstinence from the elegancies and luxuries of Mansfield Park might bring your mind into a more sober state. Is that your choice, young woman?

FANNY

Yes. It is.

General surprise.

SIR THOMAS

Why?

EDMUND

Why, Fanny?

FANNY

(very sad, without malice)

To be at home again, to be loved by my family, to feel
affection without fear or restraint, and . . . to feel myself the
equal of those who surround me could well heal every pain.

96 INT. STABLES—THAT NIGHT

Fanny says good-bye to Mrs. Shakespeare. Camera reveals Edmund watching.

97 EXT. MANSFIELD PARK FRONT STEPS—LATER
THAT NIGHT

*The carriage waits. Fanny stands before Edmund. Mary stands behind. Sir Thomas
looks on from the window but cannot bring himself to come outside.*

Edmund suddenly takes Fanny in his arms and holds her.

FANNY

Edmund, I hope you know how much I . . .

She looks at him with equal parts love and fear.

FANNY (CONT'D)

. . . shall write to you.

EDMUND

And I shall write to you, Fanny, when I have anything worth
writing about.

Fanny pulls away. Mary comes forward and embraces Fanny.

MARY

Good, gentle Fanny. When I think of this being the last time
of seeing you, for I do not know how long, I feel it quite
impossible to do anything but love you.

*Fanny, entirely surprised, cannot withstand the melancholy influence of the word
"last" and cries. Miss Crawford, yet further softened by the sight of such emotion,
clings to her with fondness.*

MARY (CONT'D)

(whispering so Edmund doesn't hear)

Who says we shall not be sisters? I know we shall. I feel that
we are born to be connected; and those tears convince me
that you feel it too, dear Fanny.

Fanny turns and leaves.

98 INT. CARRIAGE—NIGHT—MOMENTS LATER

Fanny looks out of the window.

99 EXT. MANSFIELD PARK—NIGHT—CONTINUOUS

Her POV of Mansfield Park as it recedes into the distance.

100 EXT. NORTHAMPTON COUNTRYSIDE— THAT NIGHT

The moon shines brightly. Fanny actually looks fairly content to be on her way. She pulls out her notebook and jots down a few notes. Her ride is much quieter and smoother than her first arrival at Mansfield Park.

101 EXT. ENGLISH COUNTRYSIDE—DAY—BIRD'S-EYE VIEW

The world looks lovely, in a somewhat sad way.

102 INT. CARRIAGE—DAY—CONTINUOUS

Fanny looks at herself in her hand mirror making sure everything is in place.

103 EXT. CLIFF OVERLOOKING PORTSMOUTH HARBOUR—NEXT NIGHT

The ship Fanny passed on her way to Mansfield Park is gone, but we still hear, in the distance, that SONG with a cry in it. It is fleeting, perhaps even imagined, then gone.

104 EXT. PORTSMOUTH HOUSE FRONT DOOR—LATER—MORNING

Fanny's carriage pulls up in front of Fanny's house. There is an older man slumped by the front step. Fanny gets out of the carriage and knocks on the door.

Mrs. Price comes to the door with a TWO-YEAR-OLD in her arms. She doesn't yet see the man slumped on the ground.

> FANNY
> *(excited)*
>
> Mother?

> MRS. PRICE
>
> Fanny, come, come inside. You must be exhausted from your journey.

> FANNY
>
> No, I'm fine, Mother. It is surprisingly short really.

> MRS. PRICE
> *(checking over her understatedly elegant appearance)*
> Look at you . . . so . . . so . . .

The man's hand falls off his lap into her path. Mrs. Price sighs.

> MRS. PRICE
> *(heading into the house)*
> Betsey!!! Get father up. (*to Fanny*) Come in.

It's Susy's turn!

Fanny doesn't quite know what is expected of her. She steps over him and carries her bag inside.

105 INT. PORTSMOUTH HOUSE KITCHEN—MORNING—CONTINUOUS

They step into the gray, cluttered kitchen. By the light of one small window, Fanny sees the laundry basket on the table. Last night's leftovers are still out.
Mrs. Price's voice is softly monotonous, like her sister Lady Bertram's. Only Mrs. Price's is worn by worry.

MRS. PRICE

So, did you have a tiring journey? You must be exhausted.
(*Fanny almost answers*) Betsey!

Fanny almost trips over a little boy with matted hair sleeping on some blankets on the floor. A puppy is curled up with him.

Mrs. Price hands her the laundry basket.

MRS. PRICE (cont'd)

I suppose you have a multitude of servants. . . .

FANNY

Well, I do a lot myself, I am at the right hand of Lady
Bertram and Aunt Norris. . . .

MRS. PRICE

. . . I only have the two girls. We had some but now there's
little Charlotte (*indicating little girl in her arms*) and your
father has no work at this point, so . . . (*big sigh*)

FANNY

Hello, little Charles.

Mrs. Price begins making breakfast with a heavy sigh. A 16-year-old boy bangs the door as he struts into the kitchen.

He looks her over and says nothing and is gone. Fanny stands there with the basket.

FANNY
(wondering what to do with the basket)
Where, might I . . . um . . .

MRS. PRICE
How long are you here for, Fanny?

FANNY
I cannot say, exactly. . . .

A bright-eyed girl of 18 comes down from upstairs.

SUSAN
Where is he?

MRS. PRICE
At the front.

SUSAN
She's here! Here, let me . . .

Susan takes the basket. They embrace.

FANNY
Hello, Susy.

SUSAN
Oh Fanny, you look so . . . fancy. Like a princess.

FANNY
(smiling)
Thank you.

A loud noise, Fanny jumps. Another two dirty, rosy, ragged little boys (eight and nine), come charging in yelling about a third.

SUSAN

I told you she would be beautiful, mother. Didn't I tell you
she would be beautiful?

Fanny waits for something, anything from her mother.

MRS. PRICE
(vaguely)

Yes . . . you did.

*Fanny's expectant eyes drop down to the rumpled tea towel on the top of the basket.
She folds it. And refolds it.*

106   INT. PORTSMOUTH PARLOR—MORNING—MOMENTS LATER

Mr. Price slumps into the room, supported by Susan.

SUSAN

Father, Fanny's come home, here she is.

MR. PRICE

Turn around then. Let's look at ya. (*Fanny reluctantly does*)
Lovely. Are the pretty boys already sniffing around then?
Eh? While you tinkle away on your pianoforte or titter away
in French.

FANNY

Well, um . . .

MR. PRICE
(suddenly kinder)
Come here, chatterbox, I'm just teasin' ya. Give your coarse
old father a little squeeze.

Fanny does. He hugs her a bit much for her comfort.

MR. PRICE
(holding her head in his hands)
Welcome home, Fanny.

She smiles. He lets her go.

MR. PRICE (CONT'D)
It'll be good to have another girl around. (*louder, for his wife's
benefit*) I'm about ready to just throw down some straw and
call this place a stall.

MRS. PRICE
Don't get me started.

*He sits down with the newspaper in front of the only candle in the room. Fanny
stands in the darkness. Her eyes well up. Susan sees all.*

SUSAN
Come upstairs. We shall sleep together just as we always
did.

107   INT. PORTSMOUTH BEDROOM—THAT NIGHT

Susan and Fanny sleep in spoons as they did in the beginning.

*We hear a mouse squeak, a child moaning in his sleep, then the rhythmic squeaks
of their parents' bed. Fanny tries to control her breathing so as not to reveal she is
crying. Susan wipes her sister's eyes with the sleeve of her nightgown.*

108 INT. PORTSMOUTH BEDROOM— NEXT MORNING

Fanny is reading one of her stories to Susy.

> FANNY
>
> "Beware of swoons. A frenzy fit is not one quarter so
> pernicious; it is an exercise to the body and if not too
> violent, is, I dare say, conducive to health—run mad as often
> as you choose; but do not faint—"

Betsey bursts into the room with a letter.

> BETSEY
>
> Who is it from, Fanny?

> FANNY
>
> Oh, Mary Crawford. A friend.

Slow creep in on Fanny as she reads. Fanny's voice is overtaken by Mary's.

> FANNY/MARY (VOICE-OVER)
>
> Oh how we miss you, my dearest Fanny Price. My brother
> is moping. Please write me a pretty letter in reply to gladden
> his eyes, and send me an account of all the dashing young
> captains whom you disdain for his sake.

109 EXT. WIMPOLE STREET ENTRANCE HALL—DAY

*Maria and Julia and Rushworth, still in their traveling coats, embrace Mary and
Henry and Edmund heartily.*

MARY (VOICE-OVER)

I have seen Julia and dearest Mrs. Rushworth at Wimpole Street the other day. We seemed very glad to see each other, and I do really think we *were* a little. We had a vast deal to say.

110   INT. WIMPOLE STREET DRAWING ROOM—DAY—MOMENTS LATER

They sit around chatting amiably.

MARY (VOICE-OVER)

Especially on the subject of Henry and yourself. Shall I tell you how Mrs. Rushworth looked when your name was mentioned?

MARIA

Fanny!? Fanny Price?!!!

Henry nods proudly. Maria gets up to walk and turn her face away from the group.

MARY (VOICE-OVER)

I did not use to think her wanting in self-possession, but she had not quite enough for the demands of yesterday.

Julia looks vaguely satisfied. Maria, now behind Henry, runs her finger across his shoulders flirtatiously.

MARIA

Well, I shall believe it when I believe it, Henry Crawford.

MARY (VOICE-OVER)

As for Edmund, clergyman or not, I grow more sensitive to his charms daily.

HENRY
(moving away)
And so you shall . . . Mrs. Rushworth.

111   INT. PORTSMOUTH HOUSE BEDROOM—DAY

Fanny folds up the letter and looks thoughtful.

SUSAN

What is he like?

FANNY

A rake, I think.

SUSAN

Yes, please!

FANNY

They amuse more in literature than they do in life, Susan.

SUSAN

But they amuse.

Fanny smiles, amused.

112   EXT. CIRCULATING LIBRARY—DAY

Fanny and Susan leave the circulating library carrying a stack of books.

SUSAN

And Lady Bertram?

FANNY

Well, she is always suffering near fatal fatigue.

SUSAN

Why?

FANNY

Generally from embroidering something of little use and no
beauty. Not to mention twenty-four generous drops of
laudanum daily.

SUSAN

(amused)

Your tongue is sharper than a guillotine, Fanny.

FANNY

(wincing slightly)

The effect of education, I suppose.

114   INT. PORTSMOUTH BEDROOM—DAWN—CONTINUOUS

SFX: Loud knock on the door.

BOY (OFFSCREEN)

Miss Price! Miss Fanny Price!

Fanny and Susan wake up. The boys in the next bed wake up as well.

MRS. PRICE (OFFSCREEN)

What is that racket?!

BOY (OFFSCREEN)

Miss Price!

MR. PRICE (OFFSCREEN)

What is it, boy? It is the middle of the bloody night!

BOY (OFFSCREEN)

I must see Miss Fanny Price.

115   EXT. PORTSMOUTH HOUSE—DAWN—CONTINUOUS

The neighbors look out of the window. The boy has a LARGE CRATE on a horse-drawn cart.

VOICE

What is going on?

Fanny finally appears at the door with the rest of her family. Much of the neighborhood looks on.

FANNY

I am Fanny Price.

BOY

You're sure, 'cause I don't get paid if you're not!

FANNY

I am *sure* I am Fanny Price.

BOY

All right then. Everyone stand back.

The boy nods to a companion who plays a sweet tune on the hand-organ. Boy #1 sets about lighting eight huge flares that are positioned around the outside of the cart.

The boy pulls a string which draws back the top of the crate. Five hundred white birds are released into the blue-gold sky.

Fanny and the rest of the audience look on in awe. Shouts from audience: "Look! Beautiful." SLOW MOTION on birds.

BOY #1

I was supposed to say something he said about . . . starlings flying or something, some romantic thing, but I can't remember exactly . . .

FANNY

I have got the general idea, thank you.

Fanny turns back into the house.

MR. PRICE

Fanny?! What is this?

Fanny retreats into the house.

116 EXT. PORTSMOUTH CHURCH— NEXT DAY—SUNDAY

The Price family is dressed up and just emerging from the church. Henry appears.

HENRY

Mr. Price?

MR. PRICE
(defensive)

Yes?

HENRY

(extending his hand)

Henry Crawford, a friend of (looking toward Fanny) . . .

FANNY

Edmund's.

MR. PRICE

Pleased to meet you.

HENRY

And you must be Mrs. Price, of course. I see the
resemblance to your sisters, the beautiful Lady Bertram and
Mrs. Norris. Nature has given your family no inconsiderable
share of beauty.

MRS. PRICE

You are too kind, Mr. Crawford.

Susan twinkles at Fanny. Fanny cannot help but be a little flattered by his presence.
The entire family is on their best behavior.

HENRY

(nodding toward Fanny)

Miss Price.

FANNY

Hello, Mr. Crawford.

SUSAN

It was you, wasn't it? The birds and everything.

HENRY

(slight smile)

I am sorry, I do not know to what you are referring.

Fanny rolls her eyes. He catches it.

SUSAN

It was you! I know it! Mother, it was him.

MRS. PRICE

If he says he did not do it, then we had best believe him,
Susan.

SUSAN

I know it was him.

MR. PRICE

What brings you to Portsmouth, Mr. Crawford?

HENRY

Business, sir. Tenants who have been treated ill by my agent.
I am certainly glad I decided to look into it myself, for I had
no idea they were so in need of assistance. I have found
lodging at the Crown and intend to stay a few more days.
Portsmouth is indeed a lovely town.

MR. PRICE
(favorably impressed)
Will you join us on a walk, Mr. Crawford, and see a little
more of it?

They walk off together.

117   EXT. PORTSMOUTH RAMPARTS—DAY—
MOMENTS LATER

The family walks ahead. Henry and Fanny walk together. Quiet.

FANNY

So tell me, what is the news of Mansfield? How is . . .
everyone?

HENRY

"Everyone" being . . . Edmund?

Fanny looks away as if caught.

HENRY (CONT'D)

Fanny, I know.

FANNY

You know what, Henry?

HENRY

I know you love Edmund.

Fanny cannot hide her shock.

FANNY
(recovering)
You speak so calmly what I hardly dare to tell my own heart.

HENRY

I wish to speak in truths. I suspect it is the effect of your
education of me, Fanny Price.

FANNY

I have loved him since the first day I was sent to Mansfield
Park. And he has loved me—as a sister.

HENRY

He is a fine man. I understand.

Fanny tries not to cry.

HENRY (CONT'D)

But he is to be married, Fanny, to my sister.

FANNY

The words have been spoken?

HENRY

All but.

FANNY

Then I shall try to wait to grieve until then.

HENRY

It pains me to tell you, that you must grieve now.

Fanny is silent.

HENRY (CONT'D)

I know I have an appearance of inauthenticity, Fanny Price. You are infinitely my superior in merit, you have touches of the angel in you. . . . *(Fanny looks skeptical)* And I know you have witnessed my insincere attentions toward Maria. But your eyes are so clear and unflinching, I beg you to look at me again. I am changed, Fanny Price. I am changed. I shall wait for you till the end of time. My constancy shall prove that I am changed.

FANNY

It is your very changefulness that frightens me, Mr. Crawford.

HENRY

You toy with me.

She takes his hand and holds it briefly. Their look is grave and direct.

FANNY

No. Senseless as it is, my heart is still full of another.

HENRY

Then I shall wait until it is free once more.

They walk along in silence.

118   INT. PORTSMOUTH BEDROOM—NEXT DAY

Fanny, sitting on her bed, is trying to read a letter. Her brothers are playing chase throughout the small house and the noise is deafening. We hear Edmund's voice, but it is ultimately drowned out by the racket.

119   INT. DRAWING ROOM—MANSFIELD PARK—DAY

Edmund sits at a writing table

EDMUND

It is the habits of wealth that I fear. Still, she is the only woman in the world whom I could ever think of as a . . .

His voice begins to be drowned out by children screaming.

120   INT. PORTSMOUTH HOUSE BEDROOM—DAY

Fanny can't concentrate (and we can't hear).

121 EXT. PORTSMOUTH DOCKS/BEACH—DAY— ONE HOUR LATER

Fanny walks along reading his letter.

> EDMUND (VOICE-OVER)
> She is the only woman in the world whom I could ever think
> of as a wife.

Fanny stops reading and walks along, visibly diminished by his words.

Henry enters frame. He is following her. She is aware of his presence. They walk some distance like this. Apart but aware.

She finally stops and rests against a wooden rail. He continues toward her. She feels him standing behind her. She closes her eyes.

Without looking into his face she turns to him and lays her head on his chest. Fanny weeps. Wide shot.

122 INT. PORTSMOUTH HOUSE—THAT EVENING

Close up on a glob of grisly meat in a vomitlike sauce—boiled neck of mutton. Henry sits with the family, eating. Chaos.

> MR. PRICE
> Where would your current tenants go if we were to move
> into that house?

> HENRY
> I have several apartments and houses here, sir. The others
> would be well cared for.

> MRS. PRICE
> It is a generous offer.

HENRY

The first of many I hope.

He looks to Fanny. Though embarrassed, she is not unaffected by his generosity. Fanny smiles at him, softly. He smiles back.

Fanny is the only one to notice Henry, very discreetly, trying to wipe some food flecks off of his knife. The big pot is brought to the table.

123   INT. PORTSMOUTH BEDROOM—NIGHT

Mrs. Price comes into Fanny's room. Everyone is sleeping. Fanny is trying to write by the light of the moon.

MRS. PRICE

Fanny?

FANNY

Yes?

MRS. PRICE

I've been thinking, Fanny. *(sits on bed)* There is no shame in wealth, my dear.

FANNY

That depends on how it is arrived at.

MR. PRICE (OFFCAMERA)

Hey! Where's my wife!? Frances?! Come 'ere.

Fanny and Mrs. Price look at each other.

MRS. PRICE

Just remember, Fanny, I married for love.

She gets up and leaves.

Soft gray day. Small choppy waves. Seagulls fly near the surface of the water. Fanny and Henry walk along. Their umbrella brings them together.

Susan and her younger brother walk some distance behind them.

> FANNY
>
> Look at that beauty. A ship of the line, is it not?

> HENRY
>
> I believe so.

> FANNY
>
> One would think she'd be in the Caribbean protecting our interests from the French.

> HENRY
>
> Can you see her flag?

> FANNY
>
> Not clearly.

> HENRY
>
> Well, look at that! That is most unusual! The flag on the ship. Do you see it?

> FANNY
> (squinting)
>
> No, what is it?

> HENRY
>
> Well, there is a written message where the national flag usually flies. It says, "This ship was launched . . . by the devastating smile of Miss Fanny Price." Remarkable!

Fanny pushes him out from under the umbrella but stops smiling suddenly—she sees something alarming above and behind Henry.

HENRY

What?

Henry turns but sees nothing. He looks back at her frightened expression.

HENRY (CONT'D)

What?

FANNY

Oh no! It is going to crush us! Your heavy-handed charm!
Look out.

She got him. They laugh.

They continue out toward the end of the pier.

HENRY

How does it feel to be home?

FANNY

Portsmouth is Portsmouth and Mansfield is home.

HENRY

You don't like to be near the water?

FANNY

Not if it smells . . . and one has not the means to float away
upon it.

HENRY

You do.

FANNY

Poverty frightens me, and a woman's poverty is a slavery
even more harsh than a man's.

HENRY

Arguable, but it need not be your lot.

                          FANNY

        I know.

                          HENRY

        You can spend your days in comfort. With me.

                          FANNY

        I know.

                          HENRY

        You do?

                          FANNY

        Yes.

                          HENRY

        Is that a yes?

Long pause.

                          FANNY

        Yes.

                          HENRY

        Is that "the" yes I have heard a thousand times in my heart
        but not from you? Oh Fanny Price. You will learn to love
        me. Say it again. Say it, please. Once more and forever.

                          FANNY

        Yes.

*Henry drops the umbrella, embraces her and swings her around. He stops and they
kiss. It is a deep and desperate kiss. Water all around them.*

*Another, older couple that have approached unseen in the distance look on
disapprovingly. Susan looks pleased as punch.*

125 INT. PORTSMOUTH—BEDROOM— NEXT MORNING

Fanny sits up into frame, panicked. Susan stirs beside her.

126 INT. PORTSMOUTH PARLOUR— LATER SAME DAY

CU on marigolds. Henry comes bounding in with a bouquet in hand.

> FANNY
>
> Mr. Crawford, stop. Please. I spoke hastily. I have anguished over the matter and I cannot . . . I cannot marry you. I am not prepared.

> HENRY
> *(cool)*
>
> And when might you be prepared?

> FANNY
>
> I cannot say.

> HENRY
>
> And why might that be?

> FANNY
>
> I still doubt you. I fear you cannot be trusted. Forgive me.

> HENRY
>
> Doubt *me?* And *your* behavior this day is that of someone trustworthy? *You* are the standard of trust?

His look becomes dangerously cold again.

> FANNY
>
> Henry . . .

HENRY

Enjoy your stay in Portsmouth, Miss Price. May it be long and up to your standards.

He turns and leaves.

127   EXT. PORTSMOUTH STREET—DAY

Fanny stands stunned in the street, watching Henry walk away. Susan, who has heard all, watches Fanny.

SUSAN

Are you certain, Fanny?

FANNY

I have no talent for certainty, Susy.

128   INT. PORTSMOUTH BEDROOM—DAY

Time has passed. Susan and Fanny in their room. Susan reading, Fanny writing. The hollering and door slamming from the rest of the house seems incessant.

Susan closes her book with great satisfaction. She feels its covers.

SUSAN

Astounding! I still cannot believe that we can be the choosers and renters of books. This is wealth, Fanny!

Fanny smiles and crumples up her paper.

FANNY

There is another by her you may like. . . .

MRS. PRICE

FANNY! Come quickly! FANNY!

She sees a huge pile of crumpled paper on the floor.

MRS. PRICE

Who is to pay for all this paper, Fanny?

129 EXT. PORTSMOUTH HOUSE—DAY

Fanny hurries outside to where Edmund is waiting by his post-chaise.

EDMUND

Fanny! Fanny! You must come back to Mansfield. You are
needed there.

FANNY

By whom?

EDMUND

Tom was celebrating in Newmarket and fell ill. The group
of young men he was traveling with left him behind to
recover with Yates, who then deserted him as well. Can you
imagine? He was found almost dead two days ago and
brought home. The situation is very grave.

FANNY

What is his illness?

EDMUND

I do not know. But hurry. Gather your things. If . . . you
wish to, that is.

130 EXT. PORTSMOUTH HOUSE—AFTERNOON

Fanny climbs into the carriage. Susan leans into the window.

SUSAN

Fanny, I cannot tell you how much . . .

She bursts into tears. Fanny hugs her as best she can.

FANNY

I will see you soon, Susy. I feel it.

The carriage charges down the street. Susan is the only one who watches them leave.

Fanny leans out of the window.

FANNY (CONT'D)

Remember: "Run mad as often as you choose; but do not faint—"

131   INT. CARRIAGE—AFTERNOON—CONTINUOUS

Edmund looks out of the window, lost in thought.

FANNY

I trust other than this tragedy, you are well?

EDMUND

Yes, as I intimated in my last letter, I believe Mary has almost reconciled herself to marrying a stodgy clergyman. I heard Crawford paid you a visit?

FANNY

Yes, it was brief.

EDMUND

Was he . . . attentive?

                    FANNY

Very.

                    EDMUND

And has your heart changed toward him?

                    FANNY

Yes. *(He looks at her.)* Several times. I am . . . I have . . . it's . . .

                    EDMUND

Shhhhh. *(He takes her hand.)* Surely you and I are beyond
speaking when words are clearly not enough. Let us have
the intimate luxury of silence, my love.

She smiles at him uncertainly.

               EDMUND (CONT'D)

I've missed you more than words can say.

                    FANNY

And I you, Edmund.

They ride along in silence.

132   INT. CARRIAGE—COUNTRYSIDE—DUSK

*Edmund sleeps deeply; his head droops to one side. Fanny leans nearer. Very gently
she guides his head onto her chest and cradles him there. Tears fall. He is none the
wiser.*

133   EXT. MANSFIELD PARK—DAWN

Fanny looks out to see her "home" again.

134 INT. TOM'S ROOM—MORNING OF NEXT DAY

Tom's skin is pallid and his lips are slate gray. His breathing is shallow, desperate.

Fanny comes in. Sir Thomas is sitting there, head in hands.

> SIR THOMAS
>
> Fanny, you're back.

> FANNY
> *(afraid)*
>
> Yes, sir.

> SIR THOMAS
>
> Good. That's good. We have had our fill of estrangement at Mansfield Park.

Tom laughs weakly. Suddenly he throws up in a bowl beside the bed. Edmund holds his head.

Mrs. Norris stands horrified in the dark corner of the room. Fanny leaves to get a clean cloth.

> TOM
> *(covering his eyes)*
>
> The light, please.

Edmund closes the curtains. Downstairs we hear people coming in.

Maria and Julia come in the door. They are laughing about something that happened outside, but are suddenly quieted by the somber atmosphere inside.

Fanny sees them from the top of the stairs.

> JULIA

Fanny Price, hello. How is he?

> FANNY

He is suffering. Dr. Winthrop is arriving in an hour.

Mrs. Norris appears.

> MRS. NORRIS

Oh, my dear beautiful girls. You are here. I thought Mr. Rushworth was on his way as well, Maria?

> MARIA

He is engaged with the improvements to the gardens at the moment. He should come in two days' time.

> LADY BERTRAM (OFFSCREEN)

Fanny! Please, I need you.

Fanny, happy to have a purpose, leaves quickly.

> FANNY

Excuse me.

> MRS. NORRIS

Just a moment, Fanny, how long are you staying?

> FANNY

I'm not certain, Aunt Norris. And how long are you staying?

Fanny leaves.

CU on a plate of honey and tea and toast. Fanny is just returning to Tom's room. There is a knock at the front door. There is no servant about. Fanny hesitates then puts down her tray and opens the door.

It is Henry. They lock eyes.

We see the carriage in the background with Mary in it.

> HENRY
>
> Have you told your family of our . . . conversations?

> FANNY
>
> No, I said nothing.

> HENRY
>
> To no one?

> FANNY
>
> No. My sister, Susan.

> HENRY
>
> Then that is where it must end.

FANNY

And so it shall.

HENRY

I told Mary I have chosen that our courtship shall be a
leisurely one.

FANNY
(with tenderness)
I shall not speak of it, Henry.

HENRY

Thank you.

The sadness in his eyes causes her to caress his cheek. He hears a noise and leaves
abruptly.

Mrs. Norris comes down. Mary comes in the door.

MRS. NORRIS
Hello, Mr. Crawford, Miss Crawford. Thank you for coming.
You are staying at the parsonage again with the Grants?

Fanny heads upstairs to Tom's room, carrying her tray.

MARY (OFFSCREEN)
Yes. We just came in from town as soon as we heard.

137 INT. TOM'S ROOM—NIGHT

Tom sleeps. Fanny looks out of his window.

138 EXT. STABLES—NIGHT—CONTINUOUS

Fanny's POV: Henry walks dejectedly toward the stables.

139 EXT. TOM'S ROOM—NIGHT

Medium wide of Fanny through the window as she watches Henry walk away from her. Her expression is tender.

140 INT. TOM'S ROOM—NIGHT

Tom stirs. She turns away from the window.

                    FANNY
        Tom, can I help you in any way?

He shakes his head no.

141 INT. STABLES—LATER THAT NIGHT

Henry, walking alone in the stables, suddenly comes upon Maria, who also, it seems, was intent on a solitary excursion.

                    HENRY
        Ah, Mrs. Rushworth. I trust you are well?

                    MARIA
        Fine, thank you.

                    HENRY
        And Mr. Rushworth?

Maria walks away. Henry, disturbed by her coldness, follows.

HENRY

Maria. Is this the behavior of friends?

MARIA

(cool)

Ha.

He comes up close to her, he touches her shoulder. She loves his touch.

HENRY

Maria. Please.

She turns to him.

MARIA

How is Fanny?

HENRY

She is . . . a good little girl.

MARIA

And you have become a good little boy?

They stare at each other.

HENRY

She has rejected me, Maria.

He sighs, then tries to overcome it. His emotion moves her.

MARIA

Would that this sigh was for me.

142 INT. TOM'S ROOM—THAT NIGHT

Fanny returns to Tom's room. He is asleep alone. She begins cleaning up around his bed and stumbles on his satchel. When she picks it up, a severely worn calf-bound sketchbook falls to the ground. She picks it up and sees a sketch of:

- *Detail of severely chafed wrists. Text: "Oronooko's Wrists"*

She turns a page.

- *Bunch of young white boys raping a black girl. "Our Neighbours"*

Sir Thomas appears silently behind her. He looks at the sketches with her. She is unaware of his presence.

- *Close-up on slave's face, pull back to reveal him hanging with his hands and feet tied behind him. He's hanging from a meat hook. Text: "Equiano's Last Day" (from William Blake's etching)*

- *A building out alone in a field. Text: "Slave Prison"*

- *She flips rapidly through a series of horrible sketches.*

- *She stops on a close-up of an enraged Sir Thomas with a whip in his hand.*

- *She turns to another of Sir Thomas. Seen through a partially opened door, he is standing with a slave woman on her knees in front of him, undoing his trousers.*

Suddenly, Sir Thomas grabs the sketchbook from her hands. Fanny looks at him and involuntarily steps back from him.

SIR THOMAS
He's delirious. . . . My son is mad.

He throws the entire sketchbook into the fire. She backs out of the room.

143 INT. FANNY'S ROOM—THAT NIGHT

CU fire. Fanny looks at the books in her room. Lines and voices from them are whispered as the camera passes over them. We can't quite hear what they are saying.

144 INT. SIR THOMAS'S STUDY—NIGHT—CONTINUOUS

Sir Thomas, worn by complicated grief, stares at the lithograph of Antigua. Slow creep in on his face alternating with a move in on the lithograph. Sir Thomas puts his head down and sobs.

145 EXT. MANSFIELD PARK—NIGHT—CONTINUOUS

We hear Tom's coughing. A DARK FIGURE sneaks across the lawn.

146 INT. FANNY'S ROOM—NIGHT—CONTINUOUS

Fanny hears the coughing. She pulls her robe over her white gown.

147 INT. HALLWAY—NIGHT—CONTINUOUS

As she approaches Tom's door, she stubs her toe on a small ledge and winces. She holds it in quiet pain. She opens the door quietly, lets herself in and closes it before she turns around to look inside the room.

She has let herself into Maria's room by mistake!

148   INT. MARIA'S BEDROOM—NIGHT— CONTINUOUS

Inside she sees Henry, naked, on top of a rather ecstatic-looking Maria. They haven't heard her come in. She stares open-mouthed at the scene.

Finally, she recovers enough to try to leave. The door squeaks loudly and the lovers cease their concentrated activity.

They stare at Fanny and Fanny at them. Finally she breaks the gaze and leaves.

> HENRY
> *(loud whisper)*
>
> Fanny!!

149   INT. HALLWAY—NIGHT—CONTINUOUS

Fanny almost runs/walks down the hall, covering her mouth.

150   INT. TOM'S ROOM—NIGHT—CONTINUOUS

She runs into Tom's room. Edmund is at the bedside.

> EDMUND
>
> What is it, Fanny? You look as if you have looked into the eyes of the devil! Tell me. What is it?!

Fanny cannot speak. Edmund gets up to investigate.

151   INT. HALLWAY—NIGHT—CONTINUOUS

Edmund walks toward the sound of intense whispering.

Henry then sticks his head out of Maria's door. He is wearing Maria's nightshirt.
Edmund and Henry lock eyes.

Edmund proceeds into the room to see Maria.

> MARIA
>
> Don't look at me like that! Rushworth is a fool, you know
> that, but I can't get out. . . . Edmund . . . don't . . . I can't get
> out. . . .

Edmund looks from her to Henry and finally leaves.

152 INT. TOM'S ROOM—NIGHT—CONTINUOUS

Edmund sits down beside Fanny on the love seat. He holds Fanny in his arms. Their
embrace is desperate.

> EDMUND
> (close to breaking down)
> My poor, dearest, cherished girl.

She looks up at him, he down at her. They both have tears in their eyes. Then their
mouths part as if to . . .

> EDMUND (CONT'D)
> What am I . . . ? I'm about to be engaged. . . . (he pulls back)
> . . . Forgive me.

> FANNY
> Edmund . . . I . . .

Edmund leaves. Tom wheezes and coughs.

153 EXT. MANSFIELD PARK—MORNING

The sun comes up on a crumbling wall of Mansfield.

RUSHWORTH
(cheerful)
Hello!!! Helloooo! Wake up, Mansfield!

Mr. Rushworth stands at the door with another young man.

154 INT. ENTRANCE HALL—MORNING—CONTINUOUS

Baddely lets them in.

RUSHWORTH
(full of event)
Get Edmund and Sir Thomas, and Maria. We have an
important guest here today.

Edmund comes down the hall.

RUSHWORTH (CONT'D)
Edmund, I have Mr. Dixon here from the London Times. He
is writing a feature on modern gardens and is interested in
the changes in the one at Sotherton. Where's Maria?
(bounding up the stairs) The clever fellow has noticed the
influence of Gilpin. He loves the new ruins. Wake up, you
degenerate lot!

The friend/journalist follows him.

EDMUND
Sir! Sir, please . . .

The journalist, clearly looking for more than gardening stories, chooses not to hear
Edmund calling him back.

Mr. Rushworth opens Maria's door.

155 INT. MARIA'S BEDROOM—MORNING—CONTINUOUS

It is empty.

156 INT. HALLWAY—MORNING—CONTINUOUS

Edmund stands at the base of the stairs.

> RUSHWORTH
>
> Where is Maria?

> EDMUND
>
> I cannot say.

> RUSHWORTH
>
> At this hour?

Edmund looks too tense for even Mr. Rushworth to miss the significance of her absence.

> RUSHWORTH (CONT'D)
>
> Then we'll speak to Crawford. It was on his recommendation that we removed the avenue of old oaks that leads from the west front to the top of the hill. *(pointedly)* Where is Crawford?

> EDMUND
>
> At the parsonage, with the Grants . . . ?

Rushworth stares at Edmund.

> RUSHWORTH
>
> We stopped there first.

Rushworth stares at Edmund, then looks to the newspaper man. Everyone seems to hold their breath.

157 INT. DRAWING ROOM—AFTERNOON— NEXT DAY

Sir Thomas is drinking. Lady Bertram, on the couch, is shaking her head in wonder. Edmund stares at the fire. Mary and Fanny sit at a table. Mrs. Norris rushes in.

MRS. NORRIS

Sir Thomas, there is something here you *must* read. Oh dear, dear, dear, it is quite something, here in the society section. . . .

She hands Sir Thomas the paper, he searches for his reading glasses but can't find them.

SIR THOMAS

Here Fanny, you read it for us.

Fanny takes the paper.

FANNY
(reading)
"It is with infinite concern the newspaper has to announce to the world a matrimonial 'fracas' in the family of Mr. Rushworth of Wimpole Street." Sir Thomas, are you sure you want me to . . .

SIR THOMAS

Go on.

FANNY

"The beautiful Mrs. Rushworth, who had promised to become so brilliant a leader in the fashionable world, has quitted her husband's roof in company with the well-known and captivating Mr. Henry Crawford, the intimate friend and associate of not only Mr. Rushworth but Mrs. Rushworth's father, Sir Thomas Bertram of Mansfield Park. It was not known even to the editor of the newspaper whither they were gone. . . ."

Fanny puts down the newspaper.

SIR THOMAS

May God have mercy.

MARY

The fools! Under *this* roof. They should have known Rushworth would do something stupid like bring in a newspaper man.

FANNY

Under which roof would it have been better, Mary?

MARY

I understand your bitterness Fanny Price, but do not direct it at me.

FANNY

Your brother is an actor, a charming, inscrutable actor through and through.

MARY

It is just that the temptation of immediate pleasure was too strong for a mind unused to making any sacrifice.

SIR THOMAS

After all the cost and care of an anxious and expensive education, I feel as if I do not know my own children at all.

MARY

Now please, of course you know them.

Mary gets up and walks about.

MARY (CONT'D)

This is 1806, for heaven's sakes! Forgive me if I don't forget
that this is not the first time this has happened in the world,
nor the last. Look, the deck is shuffled but the rules are the
same: Survive gracefully. You are a family in distress, but you
must recover, or lose all face and all chance of a normal life.
The facts are that if Henry does not chose to marry Maria
and if *you (indicating everyone in the room)* also reject her, she
would be an outcast.

MRS. NORRIS

A leaf in the winds of other men's plans.

MARY

Or (dramatic pause) we can recover. Here is my proposal.
We must persuade Henry to marry Maria. After a
respectable period, Edmund and I would accept Maria and
Henry into our acquaintance and . . . household.

Both Edmund and Fanny start at the implied union of Mary and Edmund.

MARY (CONT'D)

Then the rest of you, after a appropriate period of distance,
will decide to properly support them as well, and the
Bertrams, being people of respectability as they are. She
may recover her footing in society to a certain degree. In
some circles, we know, she would never be admitted, but
with good dinners, and large parties, there will always be
those who will be glad of her acquaintance; and there is,
undoubtedly, more liberality and candor on those points
than formerly.

FANNY

Such a developed strategy. And how will a poor clergyman afford these "good dinners and large parties"?

MARY

Chance is not always unkind.

FANNY

(as in "please explain")

I'm sorry?

MARY

If Tom is not able to recover, there will be *two* poor young men less in the world. Edmund will be the heir, and wealth and consequence could fall into no hands more deserving.

Everyone in the room reacts as if they were jolted with electricity.

MARY (CONT'D)

I understand you think I should not say such things. But you must prepare yourself for every eventuality; it is the mark of an evolved individual. *(Sir Thomas is about to speak.)* What I advise is that you, Sir Thomas, do not injure your own cause by interference. Let things take their course. That, I understand would be a difficult thing. But although Tom, bless his heart, may not be strong enough for this world, the rest of us must be.

Everyone in the room is speechlees.

MARY (CONT'D)

I speak merely of what must be done, not what I feel.

FANNY

You may wish to reconsider your eagerness for Tom's death.

She is startled by Fanny's quiet strength.

137

MARY

And you may wish to reconsider your thinly veiled anger
toward *me*, Fanny Price! If you had accepted my brother as
you ought, you might now have been on the point of
marriage, and Henry would have taken no pains to be on
terms with Mrs. Rushworth again. It would have all ended
in a regular standing flirtation, in yearly meetings at
Sotherton and Everingham. . . . It *could* be construed as all
your fault.

This is beyond the pale for Edmund.

EDMUND

(to Mary, quiet wonder)

Your startling adaptability to my brother's possible demise
sends a chill through my heart. A chill. You are cheerfully
planning parties with his money, you shush my father like a
dog at your table, you attack Fanny for following her own
infallible internal guide about matters of the heart. . . . All
this has most grievously convinced me that the person I
have been too apt to dwell on for many months past has
been the creature of my own imagination, not you, Miss
Crawford. You are . . . you are . . . a stranger to me. I do
not know you. And, I am sorry to say, have no wish to.

He heads out. Mary stands stunned.

158 INT. TOM'S ROOM—AFTERNOON

The doctor stands by, looking a bit helpless.

EDMUND

Is there anything to be done?

                    DOCTOR

    Wait.

                    EDMUND

    Wait.

                    DOCTOR

    Yes, time can do almost anything.

The doctor leaves and puts his hand on Sir Thomas's shoulder as he goes. Sir Thomas walks over and sits beside Tom in his bed.

                  SIR THOMAS

    He'll be all right. He survived brain fever when he was six.
    He used to play Tom the Knight. "Give me a mission,
    Father," he'd say. I'd send him with a message to Mother
    about the tea, or to get Baddeley to get the carriage ready.
    "No, Father, give me a noble mission." That's all he ever
    wanted.

Sir Thomas looks up to Fanny and Edmund, humbly, and then down again at his firstborn.

              SIR THOMAS (CONT'D)
    I'm sorry, Tom. I'm so sorry.

Close up on Sir Thomas holding Tom's hand. Fanny and Edmund look away, moved.

159 EXT. MANSFIELD PARK—AFTERNOON— CONTINUOUS

Cut to their POV: Hundreds of starlings fill one of the great oak trees of Mansfield Park.

The SEASON CHANGES FROM SUMMER TO AUTUMN. *BIG MUSIC.*

The starlings lift out of the tree, the camera takes wing: up to aerial shot of Mansfield and over hills.

160   EXT. COUNTRYSIDE—AUTUMN—DUSK

Aerial shot: We look down at the green, rolling hills.

FANNY (VOICE-OVER)
Henry Crawford chose not to marry Maria.

161   EXT. MARIA AND MRS. NORRIS'S HOUSE—AUTUMN—DUSK

Swoop down on one small house and look into the window to see: Mrs. Norris cooking.

FANNY (VOICE-OVER)
Mrs. Norris, who Sir Thomas came to regard as an hourly evil, went to devote herself to her unfortunate niece.

Maria slumps into the room and plops down at the table. Mrs. Norris irritably deposits the food in front of her.

FANNY (VOICE-OVER)
It may be reasonably supposed that their tempers became their mutual punishment.

They stop and gaze off into the middle distance for a moment as if contemplating other possible lives—

FANNY (VOICE-OVER)

It could have turned out differently, I suppose. . . .

—*then they shake their heads and return to the present.*

FANNY (VOICE-OVER)

. . . but it didn't.

162   EXT. COUNTRYSIDE—AUTUMN—DUSK

Camera lifts off again, continues over trees and lakes and arrives at:

163   EXT. MARY CRAWFORD'S HOUSE IN LONDON—AUTUMN—DUSK

Camera swoops down, looks inside and sees:

164   INT. MARY CRAWFORD'S HOUSE—AUTUMN— DUSK

Mary looks bored as Mrs. Grant serves the handsome but trivial young man beside her.

FANNY (VOICE-OVER)

Mary Crawford moved to Westminster to live with Mrs.
Grant, who was now a widow.

Henry enters the room with a pretty but equally trivial-looking young woman.

FANNY (VOICE-OVER)

And in time, Mary and Henry found partners who shared
their modern sensibilities.

SFX: Howl of wind. As Mary and Henry look off into the distance for a moment, their new partners glance surreptitiously at each other. When Mary and Henry "return," they break their flirtatious glance.

Camera lifts off again. Stark black trees on white skies.

Camera pans over to reveal (seamlessly):

165   INT. FANNY'S ROOM—NIGHT

FANNY in CLOSE-UP addressing the camera again.

> FANNY (TO CAMERA)
> . . . and, as you may have guessed, at exactly the time when it was quite natural that it should be so, and not a week earlier, Edmund ceased to care about Miss Crawford.

Tilt down from exterior of Fanny's window to a pond in front of Mansfield Park. SEASONS CHANGE in its surface. End with wall full of wisteria.

166   EXT. MANSFIELD PARK—SPRING—DAY

Tilt up to find Fanny comfortably seated with Edmund on a bench at the foot of the wall. She is writing. He is looking at her.

> FANNY (VOICE-OVER)
> It remained for a still later period to tell the whole delightful and astonishing truth.

> EDMUND
> Fanny, I must confess something.

> FANNY
> Uh-huh.

EDMUND

I have loved you all my life.

FANNY

(smiling but absorbed in her book)

I know, Edmund.

EDMUND

No, Fanny. As a man loves a woman, as a hero loves a heroine. *(Fanny gradually looks up, stunned.)* As I have never loved anyone in my entire life. *(His eyes well up.)* I was so anxious to do what is right, that I forgot to . . . do what is right.

Her eyes widen.

EDMUND (CONT'D)

What I wish to tell you, Fanny, warrants more strength of language than that in which I could possibly clothe it; for if you would, after all my blundering and blindness, choose me, it would be a happiness which no description could reach.

Fanny bursts into tears.

FANNY

Edmund . . .

Tears stream down both their faces.

Pull back further to reveal Sir Thomas and Lady Bertram out walking. They see Edmund and Fanny embracing.

> LADY BERTRAM
>
> Ah, looks like they are finally getting somewhere.

Sir Thomas smiles approvingly.

SUSAN, muttering to herself, comes out carrying the pug, which she hands to Lady Bertram. Susan seems preoccupied.

> SUSAN
>
> Now, Joan of Arc lived during the reign of Henry the . . .
> Sixth. Is that correct?

> SIR THOMAS
> *(amused)*
>
> Yes, Susy.

> SUSAN
> *(walking off)*
>
> I knew that, yes.

She wanders off, reciting to herself.

Pull back further to reveal Tom looking much healthier. He sits looking over some ledgers. Sir Thomas stops to oversee his work.

> FANNY (VOICE-OVER)
>
> Susan came to live in Mansfield Park, Tom grew stronger by
> the day and Sir Thomas eventually abandoned his pursuits
> in Antigua. He chose instead to pursue exciting new
> opportunities in Tobacco.

A tableau: Tom and Sir Thomas at the table, Lady Bertram walking, Susan making a note in a notebook, Fanny and Edmund walking arm in arm.

The wind comes up and everyone looks up for a moment. They stare and then, all together, shake their heads to rid themselves of what they were thinking and carry on in their actions. Camera lifts higher and wider, then higher and wider still. We see Edmund and Fanny walking away from camera.

EDMUND

By the way, I spoke to a John Ward at Edgerton's town and he's willing to publish, at our expense of course, but you would keep ten percent of profits.

FANNY

My stories?

EDMUND

Yes. I was thinking of a title: "Effusions of Fancy in a Style Entirely New by a Very Young Girl." Do you like it?

FANNY

Do I like it? Well, it's interesting Edmund . . .

EDMUND

Just interesting.

FANNY

But you're lovely.

Their voices fade from perception as Mansfield Park recedes from view.

THE END

Patricia Rozema quickly rose to prominence with the brilliant success of her debut feature film *I've Heard The Mermaids Singing* (1987) which won the Prix de la Jeunesse in Cannes. She went on to write and direct *The White Room* (1991) and *When Night is Falling* (1995), a critically acclaimed modern retelling of the myth of Cupid and Psyche. Her short feature *Six Gestures*, one of a sextet of short films entitled *Yo Yo Ma: Inspired by Bach*, was awarded the Golden Rose of Montreux in 1997 and an Emmy. *Mansfield Park* is her fourth feature film.

Claudia L. Johnson is Professor of English Literature at Princeton University and is the author of *Jane Austen: Women, Politics and the Novel* (University of Chicago Press, 1988); *Equivocal Beings* (University of Chicago Press, 1995) and the Editor of *The Norton Critical Edition of Mansfield Park* (WW Norton, 1998). She has published and lectured widely on film adaptations of Austen's novels and her forthcoming book, *Jane Austen: Cults and Cultures*, is about Austen's place in the public imagination.